Etched in Memory: The Elevated Art of J. Alphege Brewer

From the Library of Congress: "St. Paul's Cathedral (The Incoming Tide)" (1929), the second of Brewer's two large views of St. Paul's Cathedral from across the Thames.

Etched in Memory
The Elevated Art of J. Alphege Brewer

**An exploration of the British artist whose glorious etchings of European cathedrals
and other scenes of church, college, and community
have graced parlor walls in America and overseas for more than a century.**

Benjamin S. Dunham

Peacock Press
Mytholmroyd, United Kingdom

ISBN: 978-1-914934-13-1

Published by Peacock Press, Farm Scout Bottom Lane, Scout Road, Mytholmroyd, Hebden Bridge HX7 5JS, United Kingdom

Publisher's Cataloging-In-Publication Data
(Prepared by The Donohue Group, Inc.)

Names: Dunham, Benjamin S., author.
Title: Etched in memory : the elevated art of J. Alphege Brewer / Benjamin S. Dunham.
Description: Mytholmroyd, United Kingdom : Peacock Press, [2021] | "An exploration of the British artist whose
     glorious etchings of European cathedrals and other scenes of church, college, and community have graced parlor
     walls in America and overseas for more than a century." | Includes bibliographical references and index.
Identifiers: ISBN 9781914934131
Subjects: LCSH: Brewer, J. Alphege (James Alphege), 1881-1946--Catalogs. | Etchers--England--Biography. | Cathedrals
     in art. | Buildings in art. | LCGFT: Biographies. | Illustrated works.
Classification: LCC NE2047.6.B72 D86 2021 | DDC 769.92--dc23

On the cover: "Venice, The Doge's Palace" (1923), from the series of Blue Hour etchings by J. Alphege Brewer begun in 1921. From the author's collection, along with other images of Brewer's work used in this publication.

Text adapted from www.jalphegebrewer.info.

Images of art by Ludwig Meidner used with permission by courtesy of the Ludwig Meidner-Archiv at the Jüdisches Museum in Frankfurt am Main, Germany.

"Etched in Memory" was the title of an exhibition of Brewer's wartime etchings at the National WWI Museum and Monument in Kansas City, Missouri (https://www.theworldwar.org/explore/exhibitions/past-exhibitions/etched-memory). Used with permission.

CONTENTS

"York (Petergate)," a Blue Hour etching from 1922.

INTRODUCTION

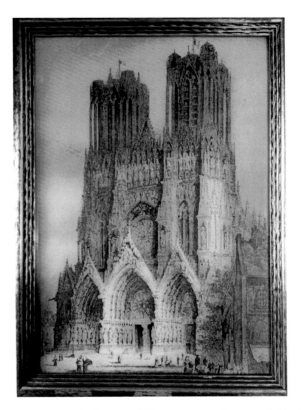

My first Brewer purchase was only a copy of a Brewer. I didn't know it was a copy when I saw it in an antique booth in New Bedford. I signaled to my wife Wendy and asked, "Doesn't this look like one of the cathedrals done by the brother of your great grandmother's second husband?"

The distant relative was the British artist James Alphege Brewer, and some years later, a family downsizing brought a few of his etchings into our home. In the process of collecting more Brewer etchings, I learned a lot about the artist and his family, and I discovered that the print I found in New Bedford was a copy of his first version of the west front of Rheims Cathedral, published in December 1914 soon after the iconic edifice had been bombed at the beginning of WWI.

It was this etching, and a companion etching of the Rheims rose windows, that made Brewer's fame as a young artist, especially in the United States. Because they weren't copyrighted in the U.S., these 1914 etchings were reprinted widely and sold at a very low cost. They became the "go to" art for thousands of people in America who were emotionally involved with the progress of the Allies, whether for cultural and patriotic reasons, or later, because they had a family member serving in the war.

I thought this might be true because of the wide availability of prints of Brewer's etchings at this time and the way they were promoted as war mementos in ads and other notices in journals and newspapers. But I had no proof, not even anecdotal evidence.

Then, listening to me talk on the phone about my latest acquisition of a Brewer cathedral, one of our dearest family friends said, "You know, I have an old print of a cathedral in my basement. It used to hang on the wall of the house I grew up in. I'll try to find it."

Sure enough, it was a copy of Brewer's 1914 "West Front of Rheims Cathedral," the same etching that made Brewer famous in this country. My friend remembered that it was practically sacred in his house. His uncle, a mentor to his father, fought in France with the American Expeditionary Forces, and he imagined that was why his parents held this print in such reverence.

He sent it to me, in its gold-leafed frame, as a gift, one that had more importance to me for what it represented than for its modest value as a print. It said something quite wonderful about Brewer's wartime etchings and the impact they had on people in this country.

Almost a year later, I was telling this story to a new acquaintance, and he remembered a framed cathedral print in his attic. It turned out be another copy of Brewer's 1914 Rheims Cathedral etching, and it had been hung in his great aunt's house. His great uncle was killed fighting in WWI, and members of his family still occasionally go to visit his grave in one of the American cemeteries in Northern France. A print that had been totally overlooked for some 40 years was now suddenly resonant with family history.

While readers may not have a Brewer etching in their attic, or even a copy of one, I hope they will experience a similar sense of discovery learning about Brewer and his life and work as an artist. I look forward to hearing about other Brewers in attics and basements and perhaps even on a few walls.

Benjamin S. Dunham, June 2021

"The Banks of Loch Katrine" (1939), among the last of Brewer's etchings published by Alfred Bell & Co. in an edition authorized by the Fine Art Trade Guild.

LIFE STORY

J. Alphege Brewer (1881–1946)

James Alphege Brewer was born July 24, 1881, in the Kensington section of London, England. He was the son of Henry W. Brewer, noted artist of historical architecture and prominent convert to the Catholic Church, and the grandson of John Sherren Brewer, Jr., editor of the first four volumes of the *Letters and Papers of the Reign of Henry VIII.* His great uncle was E. Cobham Brewer, the polymath who compiled *Brewer's Dictionary of Phrase and Fable* and authored numerous other important reference works. Among his older siblings were the artist Henry C. Brewer and the organist and writer John Francis Brewer.

James attended St. Charles Catholic College in Kensington before studying at the Westminster School of Art, where his brother Henry also trained. Other graduates of the Westminster School of Art included Aubrey Beardsley, "Jack" Butler Yeats (brother of poet W. B. Yeats), and, at the same time as James, Dorelia McNeill, the common law wife of Augustus John.

On July 23, 1910, at Our Lady of Lourdes Catholic Church on High Street in Ealing, Brewer married Florence Emma Lucas, an accomplished painter in oil and watercolor. He was not quite 29 and she was almost 41. Her great uncle was the engraver David Lucas, who collaborated with John Constable on a series of mezzotint reproductions of his paintings, and her father was the landscape artist George Lucas. "Florrie" and "Major" made their home at 106 Avenue Road in Acton, a suburb to the west of London, occupying a residence that had been in the Lucas family for a generation. Except for the duration of WWII, when they relocated to High Wycombe, Buckinghamshire, they lived their entire married lives in Acton, using the studio at the back of the property for the production of Brewer's etchings. Two brothers of Florence, Edwin and George Lucas, assisted Brewer in the engraving of the plates. While many sources say that Brewer lived in Paris for most of his working career, this is doubtful. If he resided on the Continent, it might have been at a summer base used to collect new sketches. Throughout their married lives, James and Florence were regularly listed in the London Electoral registers. The couple had no children.

In 1916, Brewer submitted a statement in support of his request for exemption from serving in World War I. In it, we have a snapshot of his personal family situation and business methods:

J. Alphege Brewer with his "The Cathedral of St. Gudule, Brussels, Belgium" (1914) on the easel.

Like many artists whose work supported family members, Brewer paid close attention to identifying subjects with a ready market.
This in part explains the many Continental and English cathedral exteriors and interiors—Milan, Rouen, Canterbury, Toledo, St. Paul's—
as well as multiple views of various colleges in Oxford and Cambridge and other scenes of interest
to tourists and readers of literature (but remarkably, almost never medieval ruins).

The Brewers on a special occasion.

The business is my own and entirely depends on me as I alone can make the plates and superintend the printing.

It has taken me 18 years to learn the work, and the work I am now doing I have invented myself and all my money is sunk into it.

I have a wife and two sisters-in-law to support, one 43 (who is very delicate and suffers acutely from lumbago and is incapable of earning her own living [probably Lily Lucas], and the other 35 [Letitia Lucas], a widow of Mr. Raleigh, who died of consumption while on Home service. I also give 15/- per week towards the maintenance of my mother, aunt, and two sisters.

The work of 8 persons besides myself is dependent on the business, one with a wife and two children.

The work is chiefly sold in America and brought into England this year over £3000 [nearly $300,000 in today's dollars] and is superseding the color printing which they used to get from Germany and Vienna.

I have between three and four hundred pounds worth of stock and orders in hand that will cover 2/3 of it and about £250 worth of debts to pay.

If the work is stopped, my business will be ruined and I will lose the American connection which has taken so much time and money to get together; also, those who assist me will be thrown out of employment.

Brewer was not exaggerating the importance of his business to the family finances. A simple calculation of the editions he was known to have produced in 1915, the year before he made this statement, shows that they could have brought in gross revenue (before expenses) of over $2 million in today's currency (though not all authorized impressions were sold in the same year). After the war, when the pound was worth less and he produced fewer large etchings, his potential revenue leveled off at about half that.

Like many artists whose work supported family members, Brewer paid close attention to identifying subjects with a ready market. This explains in part the many Continental and English cathedral exteriors and interiors—Milan, Rouen, Canterbury, Toledo, St. Paul's—as well as multiple views of various colleges in Oxford and Cambridge and other scenes of interest to tourists and readers of literature (but remarkably, almost never medieval ruins), including a large, atmospheric "Where Shakespeare Sleeps," a view of Stratford-upon-Avon signed by both James and his brother Henry. His "Liverpool Cathedral (Choir looking East)" was published in 1924 to honor the consecration of the cathedral in the presence of George V. Views of the west front of Westminster Abbey and its interior, with coronation chair in place, were issued in 1937 in connection with the crowning of

George VI. (The one exception to this general rule of thumb is "Into the Light," an experiment in religious ecstasy—see page 34.)

Sojourns in the south—trips to northern Italy and Venice—resulted in not only his usual evocative etchings of churches, palaces, and canals but also wonderful sunlit and airy views of Lake Como and Lake Lugano. These were echoed in a number of scenes from lakes in Scotland, including Loch Katrine (made famous in Sir Walter Scott's *The Lady of the Lake*) and Loch Lomond, celebrated in the song "The Bonny Banks o' Loch Lomond." In 1932, the Ealing Arts Club listed in their exhibition catalog an aquatint etching of the Taj Mahal (also hung at the Royal Cambrian Academy exhibit that same year), but other than this one example, there is no trail of etchings to indicate such peripatetic travels. Brewer may have based this etching on a photograph or perhaps a sketch or painting done by his brother Henry, whose travels included Spain and North Africa and seem to have extended at least to Cairo and Jerusalem.

Brewer exhibited at the Royal Academy (RA) and the Royal Institute of Painters in Watercolour (RI), at the Paris Salon of the Académie des Beaux-Arts, and in the shows of the Royal Cambrian Academy (RCA). He became an associate of the Royal Cambrian Academy in 1929 and a full member in the last two years of his life. He was also a member of the Hampstead Society of Artists, the Society of Graphic Art, and the Ealing Arts Club, where he was first honorary art secretary and then honorary art chairman. Florence was vice-president. Club members were once invited to a cherry picking party at the Brewer home.

The artist had some philosophical views about the nature of art and science. In April 1940, he spoke in a debate at St. Andrew's church hall as to whether science had served the best interests of man. An account said he was the first to speak from the audience and that his delivery was "breezy." It did not say on which side he spoke. In October 1943, he was at a debate about whether art should be influenced by external events. In two etchings of cathedrals done at the beginning of WWI, French flags are flying from their towers, possibly as a show of resistance. Etchings of two other damaged buildings, the Cloth Hall in Ypres and the Church of Notre Dame in Dinant, were reproduced in *The Outlook,* a New York political magazine, in 1915. In fact, Brewer's early reputation, especially in America, was built on large, color views of buildings in Belgium and Northern France that documented the devastating cultural losses

Top: "Where Shakespeare Sleeps (Stratford-on-Avon)," a 1921 etching by James Alphege Brewer and his brother Henry C. Brewer. Above: "The Taj Mahal, India," an aquatint exhibited at the Ealing Arts Club and the Royal Cambrian Academy in 1932.

If Brewer's first big success as a young artist came with etchings of buildings damaged during WWI,
as an older artist, during WWII, his approach was just the opposite.
He turned away from the war and focused on scenes of natural and almost spiritual beauty.

A family photograph of Brewer in later life.

inflicted by the onslaught of war. So it is likely that Brewer spoke in favor of the proposition.

Yet, if Brewer's first big success as a young artist came with etchings of buildings damaged during WWI, as an older artist, during WWII, his approach was just the opposite. He turned away from the war and focused on scenes of natural and almost spiritual beauty. Beginning in 1939, if we are guided by what he exhibited, Brewer began to produce woodcuts of mountain views and pastoral vistas, done with fresh colors and bold compositions. These are so different in effect from his architectural etchings that many people have trouble relating the two as the work of one artist. They appear to represent the swan song of British interest in making color woodcuts.

Brewer died February 4, 1946. The obituary in the next newsletter of the Ealing Arts Club described his demeanor at their annual general meeting as "overflowing with kindliness, fun and enthusiasm as always." It noted his fondness for music and attending the cinema, and continued:

> His nature was too big for pettiness or jealousy, and nothing pleased him more than to give high praise to a brother artist. He often alluded to the "Brewer temper," and it was as honest and whole-hearted as all his other qualities. Unkindness to another, calumny against the Club he cared for so much, called it forth, but most of all did eccentricity and distortion in the sacred name of Art arouse his fiercest indignation.

It was the "Brewer temper" that won him the nickname "Major" as a child. His outbursts reminded his father of an irritable chimpanzee by that name in the London Zoo. A mid-career sales booklet promoting his etchings confirmed (possibly in his own words, certainly with his approval) his feelings about "eccentricity and distortion":

> His success shows clearly that the public still prefers beauty in art; the cult of the ugly has never influenced him. He recognised its utter unimportance and has proved that it is possible to combine work of the highest class, work good enough to appeal to the collector, with a treatment and choice of subject that can be understood by the average man.

His *Acton Gazette* obituary said that on the last full day of his life he was practicing a song to be sung at a future gathering of the Ealing Arts Club. According to a member of the Brewer family, the next day "he went 'across the road' to see the doctor, came home, and at some point on the same day, sat in a chair and died." He was 64.

"Lake Como (Menaggio)" (1925). Sojourns in the south—trips to northern Italy and Venice—resulted in not only Brewer's
usual evocative etchings of churches, palaces, and canals but also wonderful sunlit and airy views of Lake Como and Lake Lugano.

Brewer's etchings began to appear shortly before he married into the artistic Lucas family in 1910. There are only a few illustrations in *The Girl's Own Paper* to give us a glimpse of his first published art, but a very large (his largest) "West Front of Ratisbon Cathedral" was exhibited at the Royal Academy in 1909.

In 1911, an untitled view of Ely Cathedral was included in a set of six etchings by different artists published by H. R. Howell. In the same year, the archives of the Printsellers' Association show an entry for "Aix La Chapelle," and in 1912, for "Ely Cathedral" (actually inscribed "The Octogen [sic] Ely Cathedral"), both published by Alfred Bell. A pamphlet disseminated by Alfred Bell & Co. shows five early etchings, including these two and three others in editions not listed by the Printsellers' Association.

Early on in Brewer's career, the *Fine Arts Journal* noted that his etchings were distinguished "not only as picturesque subjects picturesquely handled, but also for the almost amazing accuracy of architectural detail." The magazine went on to say that the artist "makes a picture of what in less skillful hands might degenerate into a mere architectural drawing." (Brewer must have liked this comment because it was reused in a later sales booklet.) An ad for Closson's art gallery in the March 21, 1915, edition of the *Cincinnati Enquirer* labeled him "the master of them all."

Brewer almost always included active figures as part of his architectural scenes—choristers, tourists, workmen, carters—adding a note of humanness to what would otherwise be a sterile, if often dramatic, impression. The personalities of these figures, however, never call attention to themselves and away from the settings of architectural or cultural beauty they inhabit.

Almost all of Brewer's larger etchings were published by Alfred Bell & Co. in London and marketed by subscription in limited editions authorized by the Printsellers' Association (PA) and its successor, the Fine Art Trade Guild (FATG). Their dates are given in tiny copyright inscriptions at the very bottom of each plate. In the margin underneath the image at the lower left, these etchings have either a single oval stamp (PA) or a series of five stamps (FATG) in which a letter code (now lost) indicates the numbering of the etching in the edition. (The number of etchings sold might actually be less than the number authorized, depending upon subscription demand and subsequent orders.) Editions were priced from 2 guineas to 8 guineas for the largest color etchings. For instance, the etching "St. Paul's Cathedral (The Incoming Tide)" on the frontispiece, priced at 8 guineas in 1929, would cost about $450 in today's U.S. currency.

Most of Brewer's largest color etchings were done in the decade between 1911 and 1921, and the majority of these were vertical views of cathedral exteriors and interiors. The largest of these solo productions seem to be "The Rose Windows, Rheims Cathedral," copyright 1916, and an exterior view of Amiens Cathedral published in 1918. These both measure 470 square inches in area. (An interior view of the Toledo Cathedral on which he collaborated with his brother Henry is larger still by a few square inches.) The most strongly vertical of the larger color etchings seem to be views of the north and south transepts of the cathedral in Rheims. In the 1920s and 1930s, perhaps because of changes in market tastes and in the economy (even in the availability of large copper plates), Brewer's etchings generally stayed under 350 square inches in area, except for a few views of the most popular, iconic cathedrals, like Rheims and St. Paul's. The last of the etchings published by Bell—"The Banks of Loch Katrine," and "Loch Lomond (and Ben Lomond)"—were copyrighted and recorded by the FATG in 1939.

It is difficult to date the etchings produced in the Acton studio that were not published by Alfred Bell & Co. One clue might be that Brewer, on his datable etchings, began incorporating the title into the plate in 1926. While not conclusive, this fact would be a good place to start in grouping the etchings into earlier and later periods. Most of the etchings believed to be from this later period were under 50 square inches in area. A 1925 sales booklet that seems to have been published by Brewer for the American market helps in this sorting by date.

Some of Brewer's etchings were extremely popular, requiring new versions when demand exceeded the size of a limited edition. This resulted in two very similar views of Antwerp and its cathedral from across the Scheldt and two views of St. Paul's Cathedral from across the Thames, both pairs with minor changes in positioning. There are at least six larger views of the west front of the Cathedral of Notre-Dame in Rheims. Each shows a slightly different angle of view or mode of dress. One was published in 1919 with what looks to be a peasant woman in traditional dress in the foreground. A very similar view, but with short-skirted tourists, was published in 1928. Two other views date from 1916 and 1921: one straight-on view with tourists, signed by both James and Henry, and another from about two yards to the right with figures in traditional dress. A fifth one, the first, done in 1914, was paired with an

Above left: Rheims Cathedral in a view published in 1919. Above right: the same view updated in 1928. Notice the tourist wearing a modern skirt and the correction in perspective to the statue of Joan of Arc.

interior view of the rose window at the west end, and this practice continued with the other west front etchings. The 1914 etching, like a sixth done in 1925, does not show the Dubois bronze statue of Joan of Arc in front of the west entrance. Had Brewer used a photograph taken before 1896, when the statue was installed? The west towers are both flying French flags, possibly as a patriotic gesture.

Brewer's favorite subject was the city of York, with at least 31 identified etchings (so far) of the Minster and various other scenes. Other favorites were Venice, with 17 etchings,

Above, Brewer's "Ypres," a war etching from 1915 showing the Belgian town's medieval Cloth Hall, which had been severely damaged at the war's beginning and completely destroyed by the war's end.

Rheims Cathedral, with 16, and St. Paul's Cathedral, Oxford, and Cambridge, with 10.

Beginning as early as January 1914, almost all of Brewer's etchings were large, color views of cathedrals and other historical buildings whose locations in Belgium and Northern France traced the advance of German armies at the beginning of World War I and followed developments in the continuing conflict. These included cities like Brussels, Antwerp, Ypres, Verdun, Amiens, and even Venice but also smaller Belgian towns like Dinant, Huy, and Namur. It seems that Brewer may have anticipated the onset of war and provided himself with photographs to document the appearance of these architectural wonders before they were damaged or destroyed. Reproductions of these etchings, especially two early views of Rheims Cathedral, contributed to his rising fame in America.

In the early 1920s, Brewer began to issue a series of extraordinary vertical etchings. These reproduce the luminescent, glowing sky of the "blue hour," capturing moments just after the sun has set and before full darkness has closed in. Most of them show the tower of a church or cathedral—Durham, St. Paul's, Exeter, the church of St. Jean Baptiste in Namur, York Minster, etc.—looming over a lit street in the foreground. There are a few others with the same deep celestial effect—for instance, three views from Venice, one of the Bridge of the Rialto, one of the Bridge of Sighs, one of the Doge's Palace—but the similarity of the multiple vertical tower views is striking.

Some 15 of the etchings published by Alfred Bell were co-signed. All but four of these

collaborations took place in the period after Brewer's appeals for exemption from serving in WWI had been exhausted. (He served as an Air Mechanic [draftsman] in the Royal Air Force until the end of the war.) In his absence, assistance from members of his family would have been needed to maintain a production schedule. Most of these etchings appear to be titled in pencil by someone other than James.

Nine in this period (including two published in 1919 that may have been begun before James was demobilized) were co-signed by his older brother Henry C. Brewer, whose fame as an artist preceded James's and perhaps even exceeded it. Most of these etchings show scenes in Spain, a country depicted in many of Henry's paintings.

Two etchings were co-signed by "F. Sherrin Brewer," who is listed at the Fine Art Trade Guild not as an artist but as an engraver and whose identity remains uncertain. There is no member of the immediate Brewer family whose first name begins with "F" and whose middle name is "Sherrin" (or, as it might be, "Sherren," the correct spelling of Brewer's great-great grandmother's maiden name). James's sister Frances Anna was a barrister's wife with three young children. His mother Frances might have stepped in to help, but she was in her mid-70s. While it is possible that his wife Florence used "Sherrin" to distinguish these efforts from her own well-regarded paintings, signed "F. Lucas Brewer," an examination of the available signatures strongly suggests that the co-signer was James's brother Edward, whose own etchings have the same fine-line exactitude.

Top: "Evening on the Meuse. Huy," a 1916 collaboration of J. Alphege Brewer and "F. Sherrin Brewer" (Edward Brewer? See signatures above).
Far right: "La Rue de la Grosse-Horloge, Rouen," one of the striking Blue Hour etchings Brewer produced in the early 1920s.

EARLY ART

*Each of these confirms
drawing skills that would
certainly pass examination at a
school like the Westminster School
of Art, where Brewer had recently studied,
but they don't exhibit an individual
viewpoint or personal artistic stamp.
Were these paintings typical of what
Brewer was producing on his own,
or do they represent only what
The Girl's Own Paper
commissioned him to paint?*

A number of illustrations by James Alphege Brewer in *The Girl's Own Paper* contribute to our understanding of his art in the years before his first etchings began to appear.

The Girl's Own Paper was started in 1880 by the Religious Tract Society (later Lutterworth Press) to edify and entertain daughters in middle- and upper-class families. From early on, members of the Brewer family were involved. The first was James's great aunt by marriage, Emma Brewer (née Rose), who wrote on a wide range of topics, including hospitals, servants, the making of perfumes, and the Bank of England. Then his father, Henry William Brewer, wrote numerous articles on historical architecture. His older brother, the organist and writer John Francis Brewer, collaborated with the editor Charles Peters on travelogues describing trips they took together to Italy and Norway in 1887–88.

In the period 1905–08, *The Girl's Own Paper* published four color plates of Brewer paintings, and also a series of four black-and-white illustrations for a serialized "Romance of the Norlan' Seas" by W. Gordon Stables.

The color plates were bound into editions in 1905 and 1907 as frontispieces to the monthly numbers, and each is a romanticized view of young womanhood of a kind that is typical of this publication. "Come Back to Erin" portrays a red-haired lass in a lace-trimmed robe playing the harp, and "A Bed of Daisies" shows a young mother (we can assume) in a field of flowers exchanging adoring looks with her baby. In "Summer," a bonneted young lady admires a nosegay plucked from the wildflowers bordering her path. In April 1907, Brewer supplied another frontispiece, this time a contemplative young woman in an oval frame illustrating the Christopher Marlowe verse, "By shallow rivers to whose falls/Melodious birds sing madrigals" (slightly misquoted as "O by rivers by whose falls...") from "The Passionate Shepherd to His Love."

Each of these confirms drawing skills that would certainly pass examination at a school like the Westminster School of Art, where Brewer had recently studied, but they don't exhibit an individual viewpoint or personal artistic stamp. Were these paintings typical of what Brewer was producing on his own, or do they represent only what *The Girl's Own Paper* commissioned him to paint? In the Marlowe painting, there are indeed "shallow rivers" but no "falls" and no "melodious birds," so we may suspect that the quote was chosen to fit an existing painting and not the other way around.

The four illustrations for the Gordon Stables romance present a different picture. One who hadn't seen the academically accomplished frontispieces from earlier years would think that these 1908 drawings revealed a worrisome nescience of anatomy and physiognomy (even the castle disappoints). But surely Brewer was attempting to match the archaic language of the romance with a deliberate "folk" style in keeping with the mythic culture of the characters in the text. Was Brewer influenced in these drawings by the work of emerging international artists in which photographic accuracy of anatomy, facial expression, and perspective is less important than the overall

Above: four Brewer frontispieces printed in *The Girl's Own Paper, 1905–07*. Below: Brewer's 1908 illustrations for "Romance of the Norlan' Seas" by W. Gordon Stables.

NONSUCH HOUSE.
From the Painting by H. W. and Alphage Brewer.

"Nonsuch House" on London Bridge, a 1908 illustration by J. Alphege Brewer and his late father, Henry W. Brewer.

mood? It is unlikely that Brewer would have seen works by Chagall (who would have been 21 in 1908). But he was the same age as Picasso, and Matisse and Munch were well established. It is not unlikely that a young artist in Britain would experiment at this time with what was important in an artwork and what was not.

As one observer has noted, "What jumps out at me are the mountains! High snow-clad mountain peaks. Clean, clear, champagne air. Then you think of his woodcuts of majestic mountains and his etchings of scenes in northern Italy and the Scottish lakes. That is what he dreamt of while having to comply with the strict social straitjacket of Edwardian London—higher, cleaner ethereal beliefs reflected in the sheer majesty and power of the majority of his etchings."

A clue to Brewer's future appears in another color frontispiece from 1908: "Nonsuch House," a reconstruction of what London Bridge looked like before the bridge's buildings were removed after 1757. It is attributed jointly to Alphege Brewer and his father, the well-known illustrator of historical architecture Henry W. Brewer, who had died five years before, in 1903. If they worked on this painting together, the father might have been trying, helpfully, to lead his son to follow in his footsteps. If it was an unfinished painting completed by Alphege Brewer, perhaps this was the son's posthumous acknowledgment of where his talents really lay. A year later, his massive etching "West Front of Ratisbon Cathedral" was exhibited in the Black and White Room at the Royal Academy in London.

WARTIME ETCHINGS

From 1914 to 1919, Brewer published many large, color etchings showing scenes from Belgium and Northern France—cathedrals, churches, and town buildings threatened or damaged during the battles of World War I. Both in the United States and Great Britain these etchings, and inexpensive copies of them, were proudly hung on parlor walls in solidarity with the Allied cause and as a remembrance of the devastating cultural losses inflicted by the onslaught of war.

Brewer's wartime etchings showed the historic buildings as they once were, not as they appeared after the attacks. They must have been sketched or photographed before the war began, a fact suggested in a December 1915 edition of the New York political journal *The Outlook*: "These etchings were made shortly before the war and are worthy memorials of magnificent edifices which are now partly or wholly in ruins." Brewer would likely have seen newspaper articles in 1913 about the course of a possible invasion of Belgium. For instance, in September 1913, after the Belgians had finished their summer training war games, the Paris correspondent for *The Times* reported that the French grumbled about the defensive exercises near Dinant and Namur, a course that was "considerably to the north of that which a German army would follow if it violated Belgian neutrality." But only a year later, that was exactly where the Germans

attacked. Reading reports like this, Brewer might have known enough in 1913 to envision a series of etchings showing scenes from the heart of Belgium. As Barbara Tuchman pointed out in *The Guns of August*, the Schlieffen Plan (even with Moltke's adjustments) was based on a German advance through the whole of Belgium. Schlieffen said, "Let the last man on the right brush the Channel with his sleeve."

Brewer's most prolific year was 1915, when Alfred Bell & Co. published 13 of his etchings, 11 of them scenes of places that had been destroyed or were in danger from the events of the war. A March 1915 ad for Closson's art gallery in the *Cincinnati Enquirer* was headlined "Etchings from Warring Europe," and the text continued, "We have just received about a dozen new subjects by Mr. Brewer, some of which were sketched in cities mentioned in the war despatches of recent months." More would follow throughout the war. Sixteen of them, described as "places and buildings mutilated by the Germans during the great European War," were listed in 1918 as additions to the holdings of the museum of the Royal United Service Institution in London. As a group, these etchings—which were, in essence, anti-war or, at the very least, nostalgic for an earlier era of peace—argue for their inclusion in surveys of important and influential political art.

The Cathedral of St. Gudule, Brussels, Belgium.
Published in January 1914, this etching of the cathedral in Brussels may represent an artistic premonition that foreign troops would soon march in the streets of Brussels (see photo). There had been many published reports predicting hostilities that were especially worrisome for those with a concern for Belgium. Some examples: In January 1913, *The Times*'s military correspondent had written that Belgium had "no natural obstacles to present to an invader." In April 1913, the paper's German correspondent reported "the fear prevailing in Belgium that Germany might violate her neutrality in the event of war." Then in September, a *Times* article warned that planning for a proposed channel tunnel might be premature "at a moment when the probability of a German offensive through Belgium is so seriously exercising Continental strategists." Finally, a review of the military novel *In the Cockpit of Europe*, printed in *The Observer* in November, praised its author as a "master of the military detail demanded for the battles to be fought...very near Liège, where France and Germany are to be the combatants, with England as the ally of the former in defending Belgium against invasion." Because a U.S. copyright was not included, litho copies of this etching were sold widely in America. Were the French flags flying from the towers an expression of Brewer's own sympathies or rather a concern that Belgium might come under French control? We don't know; this was certainly not a reflection of the official Belgian policy of neutrality.

"Beside the temple of religion we erect the fortresses of destruction.

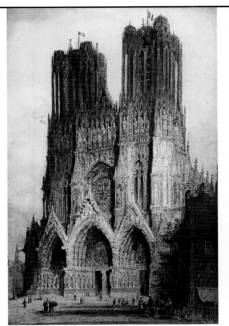

The West Front of Rheims Cathedral and **The Rose Windows Rheims Cathedral.** At the beginning of the WWI, Brewer completed his first etchings of the west front and rose windows of the Cathedral of Notre-Dame in Rheims, the iconic site of the coronation of Charles VII in 1429 after Joan of Arc's victories over the English. The cathedral had been shelled in September 1914. The timing of publication, December 1914, and the French flags flying from the towers leave no doubt about the message Brewer was trying to impart. It was these two etchings, also published without a U.S. copyright, that Emil Jacobi and others reproduced and marketed widely to an American public sympathetic to the Allied cause.

Rheims Cathedral and **The Rose Windows, Rheims Cathedral.**
A new version of the West Front of Rheims Cathedral, co-signed by James and his brother Henry, was published in 1916 in an edition of 500 (largest yet of any Brewer edition). This time it included the statue of Joan of Arc that had been missing from the 1914 etching. We can only guess that Henry realized that his brother had used an old photograph of the cathedral for his first etching of the West Front, one taken before the statue had been installed in 1896. (If James had gone to Rheims anytime after 1896, he would have seen the statue.) Like the earlier etching, this new version was also widely distributed in a litho print.

Within the shadow of the cathedral we build the barracks of the professional soldier.

Rheims Cathedral from the South West. Another etching of Rheims Cathedral, published in 1917, together with a photo showing its roof in flames during shelling on September 19, 1914. Michelin's post-war guide for Rheims reported that a dozen injured German soldiers being cared for in the cathedral died when the roof collapsed.

Nave Looking East, Rheims Cathedral. An etching of the interior of Rheims Cathedral published in 1916, along with a photo showing the rubble in the chancel after the vaulting collapsed.

Hôtel de Ville, Louvain. In 1915, Brewer pictured the 15th-century town hall in Louvain, Belgium, near the historically priceless university library, which was burned by German troops.

Mingled with the Hosannas to the Most High can be heard...

Malines. A view of St. Rumbold's Cathedral and the Grote Markt square in Malines (Mechelen), Belgium, published in September 1915. Malines came under attack in the first weeks of the war. The secretary to the U.S. legation in Brussels wrote: "...the Cathedral...is a dreadful sight, all the wonderful old 15th-century glass in powder on the floor.... A few of the surrounding houses...were completely wiped out...."

Antwerp and **Antwerp Cathedral.** A waterfront view of the city of Antwerp, Belgium, published in May 1915, and a view of its cathedral with the statue of Rubens to its south, published in 1917. The city was attacked in the early months of the war, first with bombs dropped from a Zeppelin airship (Count von Zeppelin pictured in the German postcard) and then with artillery fire during the Siege of Antwerp. In an unpublished manuscript, Edouard Bunge, a merchant in Antwerp, remembered: "Everywhere one looked, one saw flames appearing above the housetops, one heard the shells whistling over, and the roar of their explosions together with the crash of falling walls made a great and terrible combination. One felt powerless—at the mercy of some irresistible force let loose." (transl., Milton M. Brown) Germans were given maps showing cultural sites to avoid, but nevertheless, the cathedral's south transept windows were damaged.

Evening on the Meuse. Huy.
Published in September 1916. After the bridge over the Meuse was blown up by the retreating Belgian Army, the city of Huy was attacked by the 2nd German Army under Karl von Bülow on its way to Namur. To cross the Meuse, the Germans built a temporary bridge.

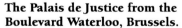

On the Sambre, Old Namur.
Published in 1914. In the top right corner, Brewer pictured the foundations of the Citadel of Namur, part of a system of forts that were of little help in defending against the 2nd German Army. The contrast between this peaceful canal scene and the devastation pictured in the postcard of the German soldier posed in the rubble of the Place d'Armes—located behind the houses to the left—is startling.

The Palais de Justice from the Boulevard Waterloo, Brussels.
Published in October 1915, this etching issued an indirect but firm reprimand for the German occupation of the capital of Belgium. A notable landmark in Brussels, the Palais de Justice is larger than St. Peter's Basilica in Rome and is said to be the largest building constructed in the 19th century. The photo shows German soldiers fraternizing in its Court of Appeals.

the clang of the hammers shaping instruments of death.

The Church of Notre Dame, Dinant-on-the-Meuse, Belgium and **Ypres.** These two etchings of scenes in Belgium, one of the medieval Cloth Hall in Ypres and one of the interior of the Church of Notre-Dame, Dinant, were reproduced in a December 1915 issue of the influential American political journal *The Outlook* under the headline "Architectural Sacrifices of the Great European War."

Hôtel de Ville, Arras. Brewer's 1917 etching of the town hall in Arras, France: The area around this historic 16th-century building was bombed three times during October 1914, leaving the town looking like "a modern Pompeii."

Laon Cathedral. The Cathedral of Notre-Dame of Laon, France, an etching that was co-signed with James's brother Henry and published in September 1917 when James was serving in the armed forces. In the fall of 1914, German forces captured the town and held it until the Allied offensive in the summer of 1918. The photo shows captured French soldiers by the city walls of Laon with the cathedral in the distance.

Verdun from the Meuse. Published May 1, 1916. The Battle of Verdun, lasting from February 1916 to the end of the year, was the longest of World War I. When the German initiative was finally called off in order to reinforce troops in the Battle of the Somme, Verdun and the surrounding area were left severely damaged.

Church of the Holy Sepulchre, Jerusalem. After Gen. Edmund Allenby captured Jerusalem from the Turks in December 1917, he entered the city on foot and issued a proclamation that included: "The hereditary custodians at the gates of the Holy Sepulchre have been requested to take up their accustomed duties...." Henry and James collaborated on an etching signifying the event in August 1918.

Amiens Cathedral. Pictured in an etching published in September 1918, the cathedral in Amiens is the largest Gothic structure in France. In August, the Battle of Amiens began the Allied counterattack that led to the end of the war. While the cathedral survived mostly intact, on May 4 a shell crashed into the Chapel of St. John the Baptist (see photo).

and the groans and petitions for mercy from the agonized lips of the vanquished."

—James A. Reed (1861–1944),
U.S. Senator, Missouri

Other "wartime etchings" include one of the Church of St. Gertrude in the occupied town of Louvain as well as scenes from Bruges and Dieppe. In addition, two etchings of buildings in Venice—an interior of St. Mark's Basilica (1915; see page 42) and an exterior of the Doge's Palace (1916)—might be counted as war etchings. Austria bombed the Piazzetta di San Marco and other sites during this period, as noted by Alan Kramer in his *Dynamic of Destruction*, "in the hope, as the Germans had in destroying Rheims cathedral, of intimidating Italy with the fear of the mortal danger thus facing its 'città adorabile.'"

The North Transept, Rheims Cathedral and **Ypres [Cloth Hall].**
At the beginning of 1918, Brewer's series of etchings revisited two sites, the Cloth Hall in Ypres and Rheims Cathedral, both of which had suffered repeated attacks throughout the war. The new Cloth Hall etching was co-signed by "F. Sherrin Brewer" (his brother Edward?) when James was serving as a draftsman in the RAF.

The art of Ludwig Meidner and J. Alphege Brewer in 1910 before they went in different directions. Top: J. Alphege Brewer's "Charing Cross As It Looks Today," published in *The Graphic*. Above: Ludwig Meidner's "Bau der Untergrundbahn in Berlin" (Subway Construction in Berlin). Note that where Meidner places a derrick, Brewer centers Nelson's Column.

During WWI, Brewer's imposing etchings of cathedrals, city views, and medieval town halls in Belgium and Northern France implicitly warned of threats to their existence and in some cases lamented their destruction. But how well did they fit with other artistic currents of the time?

In a 2014 article in *The Guardian,* Margaret MacMillan, author of *The War That Ended Peace,* wondered if artists like Picasso and Braque and writers like Henry James and Marcel Proust "somehow felt a catastrophe was bearing down on them and their societies.... For some," she wrote, "war and violence were not things to be feared but welcomed, as ways of speeding up the destruction of the old and the outworn. War, said the Italian futurist Marinetti, 'is the sole hygiene of the world.' Rupert Brooke longed, he told his friends, for 'some sort of upheaval.'" In music, as Marc Swed has written in *The Los Angeles Times*, "With [Arnold Schoenberg's 1912] *Pierrot lunaire*, as far as scandalized contemporary critics were concerned, a hallowed art form, the soul of European civilization, was on the sure track to self-destructive anarchy."

An artist like Brewer, with a love of history and historical architecture, might have agreed with the critics of *Pierrot lunaire*. Certainly, his patrons would not warm to the idea of tearing down what the ages had passed on as a legacy. (Except for "Barnard Castle," remarkably, Brewer is not known to have done etchings of the many well-visited medieval ruins in Britain.) Other young artists might have welcomed a violent new beginning, but as a member of a family that included the editor of Henry VIII's letters, an architectural historian, a church organist, and the polymath author of *Brewer's Dictionary of Phrase and Fable,* Brewer would have anticipated the onset of a destructive war with deep trepidation.

The German expressionist Ludwig Meidner was on a different path. At 17 he had been apprenticed to a stonemason, and his early scenes of Berlin buildings exhibited a workmanlike firmity, not much different from an early Brewer drawing in *The Graphic*. But in 1912, perhaps influenced by the dystopian poetry of his colleague Georg Heym, he began a new series characterized by screaming comets, twisted architectural forms, frenzy, and disruption. In contrast, a eulogy for Brewer in the newsletter of the Ealing Art Club stressed that "most of all did eccentricity and distortion in the sacred name of Art arouse his fiercest indignation."

In his book *Dynamic of Destruction: Culture and Mass Killing in the First World War,* Alan Kramer thought Meidner's visions "by no means expressed enthusiastic anticipation of war, rather dread and horror." Sophie Goetzmann, however, sounded a cautionary note. "Far from being prophetic," she wrote in a chapter of *Wounded Cities, The Representation of Urban Disasters*, "these visions of disaster and destruction were primarily the symptom of intergenerational conflict, and an aspiration to provoke radical change in the world order." And Jay Winter, in *Sites of Memory, Sites of Mourning*, agreed: "It was class war and not international conflict which loomed on the horizon."

Meidner's paintings and drawings from this period were exhibited together as *The Apocalyptic Landscapes of Ludwig Meidner* in 1989 at the Los Angeles County Museum of Art. The excellent catalog text by Carol S. Eliel traces the influences on Meidner's evolution as an artist, including the work of earlier German expressionists and, in addition to the poetry of Heym, the writings of Friedrich Nietzsche. But Nietzsche's "O Zarathustra, spit on this city of shopkeepers and turn back" would have had little appeal for an essentially bourgeois artist like Brewer (although this aspect of his art is belied in his exceptional "Into the Light" from 1933; see page 34).

As pictured in the catalog, most of Meidner's paintings and drawings seem to be an expression of post-*fin-de-siècle* angst, a vision of social and architectural upheaval rather than a depiction of world war, even the paintings done after the war had begun. Indeed, as late as a June 1914 article in *Kunst and Künstler*, Meidner talks about "a bombardment of light beams whizzing between the rows of windows, between vehicles of every kind, and a thousand bobbing balls, scraps of people, billboards, and roaring shapeless masses of color"—without reference to any impending military conflict.

Writing his post-war autobiographical *Mein Leben,* however, Meidner linked his pre-war art to the "great universal storm...already baring its teeth." While Goetzmann found nothing he wrote before the war to corroborate such an interpretation, those looking for a military cause for all this teeming terror and devastation can point to Meidner's 1913 "Bombardement einer Stadt" (Shelling of a City). This drawing shows a city flashing explosive lights under cannon fire and is certainly consistent in style and subject with his 1914 "Schlacht" (Battle). Meidner was at least including the possibility of armaments in his fevered, apocalyptic visions.

Above: Ludwig Meidner's 1912 "Apokalyptische Landschaft." Below: his 1913 "Bombardement einer Stadt."

During the war, artists like Paul Nash, Otto Dix, Natalia Goncharova, David Bomberg, CRW Nevinson, Henry Tonks, William Orpen, Georges Rouault, and many others depicted images of grief, conflict, and ruin that made important contributions to public awareness and understanding, even as Brewer's brother Henry did in his paintings of the bombing of London during WWII.

In 1917, Brewer was called up to serve as a draftsman in the newly formed RAF, but with the help of family members, the production of his war etchings continued. At the same time, some American artists enlisted their talents as captains in the Army Corps of Engineers and were given free rein to capture the essence of war. "They could go anywhere they wanted to go," according to Alfred Cornebise, author of *Art from the Trenches: America's Uniformed Artists in World War I.* While the results included scenes of soldier life and combat as well as destroyed churches and devastated fields, the artists stopped short of showing any dead bodies like those piled up in the foreground of Meidner's 1918 postcard illustration "Schlachtfeld" (Battlefield).

Above: George Bellows's 1918 painting "Massacre at Dinant." At right: Brewer's 1915 "The Church of Notre Dame, Dinant-on-the-Meuse, Belgium." While Brewer's etching is reverent and soothing, its impact was not inconsiderable.

A telling point of comparison with Brewer's art can be made with the work of American artist George Bellows. In 1918, Bellows created a series of evocative tableaux—five large oils and multiple prints and drawings—titled *War.* These documented the German invasion of Belgium in 1914. His execution scene from Dinant—a painting with much the same wrenching emotional power as Picasso's "Guernica"—presents a stark contrast with Brewer's serene memento of the interior of Dinant's Church of Notre Dame, shown as it existed before the German offensive blasted its way through the town on the way to France. While Brewer's etching is reverent and soothing, its impact was not inconsiderable. Said to have been done before the war began, it was published in 1915 as the world was still reeling in disbelief after reading reports of the invasion. When it was reprinted at the end of that year in *The Outlook,* together with the etching of the Cloth Hall in Ypres, they were praised by the influential political magazine as "worthy memorials of magnificent edifices which are now partly or wholly in ruins." In contrast, after the war, art critic Virgil Barker wrote that the paintings in the Bellows series were as "ill-judged in their appeal to the passion of hatred as anything produced in America's most hysterical war years...."

In this context, despite art prints being nominally among Marshall McLuhan's "hot" media, we can value the "cool" quality of Brewer's war etchings—artwork that invites, even requires, a high degree of viewer involvement for its full impact. They are quietly symphonic—exhibiting scale, color, technique, approachability—and quite different in effect from the chamber music played by the works associated with the "etching revival," with their more personal artistic language. Think *A London Symphony* by Vaughan Williams, not *Pierrot lunaire.*

During the war, Brewer published seven etchings of Rheims Cathedral, whose destruction was an architectural rallying cry for supporters of the Allies. Each of these etchings is filled with a sense of monumental loss like that expressed in "The Goblin at Rheims," a sonnet by American poet Hortense Flexner:

From his high arch, nestled in stony nook,
He used to leer across the twilight space
Of the great aisle — the goblin with the book,
Bent in huge hands. Half lost in ivoried lace
Of shadow carving, scrolls and thick-twined
   gorse,
His savage face was sly with some dark jest;
I thought it strange he lived so cruel, coarse,
Above five centuries' drifted prayer and rest.
   To-day I knew him by his evil sneer,
In shattered rose-glass, fretwork, fallen towers;
And wondered if he told his maker's fear
Of this far shame. But no — who dreamed
   these flowers,
Modeled of light, this laughing cherub's wing,
How should he think men's hands might
   do this thing?

This same unanswerable question is asked by Brewer's subtly poignant and silently reproachful WWI etchings. In this sense, they may be appreciated as lacunae of ruin, all the more powerful in their urgency because of their restraint. As author Alan Kramer wrote in a letter, "The etchings are remarkable because they are understated, yet they would resonate strongly for viewers at the time with the knowledge of contemporary events."

What Abbé Morel said of the *Miserere* series by Georges Rouault is even more appropriate for Brewer: He had found a way "to participate in the battle by rebuilding what the battle had destroyed in man."

Below: J. Alphege Brewer's "The West Front of Rheims Cathedral." Because it was published in 1914 without a U.S. copyright, the image was reproduced by many printers and sold widely throughout the United States.

A PERSONAL REVELATION

In 1934, the Fine Art Trade Guild made an entry for a different kind of Brewer etching, unlike any he had made before or would ever make again.

Titled "Into the Light," it seems to be a one-off experiment in religious ecstasy. For precedents you must go back to Hieronymus Bosch's "Ascent of the Blessed" and the poetry and images of William Blake, and seek out other artwork of revelation and rapture. There is no hint of this kind of theosophy in Brewer's etchings of cathedrals or in the pastoral woodcuts he did in his last years, even as uplifting as these are for many viewers. There is no other instance of his moving beyond the real toward the surreal.

"Into the Light" presents a tableau of struggling humanity standing on fallen, burnt timbers and reaching for and merging with a brilliant white light shining down in the shape of a cross. The cross is wearing a crown of thorns. Everyone and everything, including the distorted, inflamed cathedral towers, are swept up to the heavens. The deformed

Top: J. Alphege Brewer's "Into the Light," copyrighted in 1933 and recorded by the Fine Art Trade Guild the following year. Left: Ludwig Meidner's 1918 "Strasse am Kreutzberg." The overt Christian imagery in the Brewer is foreign to Meidner's Nietzschean mindset; the towers are rising toward ethereal bliss rather than being twisted in psychological angst.

buildings, so unlike Brewer's usual solid architectural shapes, remind one of the warped urban images of Ludwig Meidner, done before and during WWI. But the overt Christian imagery of Brewer's etching is foreign to Meidner's Nietzschean mindset; the towers are rising toward ethereal bliss rather than being twisted in psychological angst.

It is likely that Brewer made this etching as an expression of personal faith. The Fine Art Trade Guild accepted it as an authorized edition of 300, but, at this point, it is not clear that the etching was ever put into production, or, if the etchings were made, that they were indeed marketed and sold on subscription by his regular publisher, Alfred Bell & Co. The only known copy is held by the family, and, while it is signed, it is not debossed with the FATG stamps.

The texts for the etching might be ones familiar to many people from Handel's *Messiah*:

> But who may abide the day of His coming, and who shall stand when He appeareth? For He is like a refiner's fire. (Malachi 3:2)

And four numbers later in the oratorio:

> For behold, darkness shall cover the earth, and gross darkness the people; but the Lord shall arise upon thee, and His glory shall be seen upon thee. And the Gentiles shall come to thy

*There is no hint of this kind of theosophy in Brewer's etchings
of cathedrals or in the pastoral woodcuts he did in his last years....
There is no other instance of his moving beyond the real toward the surreal.*

light, and kings to the brightness of thy rising. (Isaiah 60: 2–3)

Many observers have noticed that Brewer, almost always, focused on an area of light in his etchings as a gentle way to draw attention to a particular feature or to provide a depth of chiaroscuro to the composition. Brewer himself mentioned atmosphere and light—"'luminosity' in the parlance of the modern art critic"—in describing the effect of his etchings.

In this etching, however, the light is meant to be more than luminous; it is transfiguring. Beyond seeing a great light, the mass of humanity is actually drawn to it. In his book *Life After Life*, Raymond A. Moody, Jr., M.D., writes of the near-death experience:

> What is perhaps the most incredible common element in the accounts I have studied...is the encounter with a very bright light. Typically, at its first appearance, this light is dim, but it rapidly gets brighter until it reaches an unearthly brilliance.... He senses an irresistible magnetic attraction to this light. He is ineluctably drawn to it.... Most of those who are Christians...identify the light as Christ and sometimes draw Biblical parallels in support of their interpretation.

In the etching, one notices the atomization of the people as they float toward the celestial light, almost as if the souls become merged into the thrall of a heavenly existence, as in the common phrase "becoming one with God." See 1 Corinthians 6:17:

> But he who is joined to the Lord becomes one spirit with Him.

John Switzer, professor of theology at Spring Hill College in Mobile, Alabama, thinks "the manner in which humanity is present all the way to the top of the image certainly speaks to me of the Rapture as explained by St. Paul in 1 Thessalonians 4:16."

> Then we who are alive, who are left, shall be taken up together with them in the clouds to meet Christ, into the air, and so shall we be always with the Lord.

Brewer was named for St. Alphege, Archbishop and First Martyr of Canterbury. His father was a prominent convert to Catholicism, and his older brother John Francis Brewer was the organist at the Church of the Immaculate Conception, a Jesuit church in central London. It is possible that, beneath the surface, feelings of Catholic mysticism were strong in Brewer. In the thinking of early church mystics, a complete union with God is realized by entering the "Cloud of Unknowing," in which one can begin to glimpse the nature of the Divine.

More digging must be done into what provoked Brewer to make this etching, especially since the style and import were never repeated. Was it some world event? Or a fatidic first heart attack accompanied by a near-death experience? Was this unusual etching accepted for publication by Alfred Bell & Co.? And if so, what would have caused Bell to think that he could find a market for 300 copies?

Although the size of the etching and its coloring suggest 1933–34 as the correct date, it is possible that "Into the Light" recalled an earlier revelation of cathedral towers in flames during WWI with worshipers seeking absolution from the Almighty for the cataclysm humanity had brought upon itself. Or perhaps the etching reflects the great loss of life during the Spanish Flu pandemic in 1918–19. During and immediately after the war, such an extraordinary image would have disrupted the established market for Brewer's solemn architectural memorials, but it might have been resurrected when the embers of war had cooled. One hint: the in-plate titling, inscribed over a burnished area, looks as if it could have been added after the fact, as would have been the case with an etching originally done before 1926.

Whatever the timing or cause, the result reveals previously unknown aspects of Brewer's artistry in both style and substance.

Above: "Lake Thirlmere (& Hellvellyn)," exhibited 1939 SGA, exhibited 1945 RCA; "On the Dochart (Perthshire)"; "Lake Como (The Pergola)"
Below: "The Harvest Moon," exhibited 1945 RCA; "St. Paul's Cathedral (from Bank Side)"; "Lake Lugano."

WOODCUTS

By Gordon Clarke

Brewer was one of the very last British artists to make color woodcuts. They first appeared at the Society of Graphic Art exhibition in 1939. Presumably, he had begun to make them some time before. Color woodcuts are by no means easy to produce, but there is no sense of the beginner in the earliest ones.

Perhaps Brewer knew the work of John Platt and his book, *Colour Woodcuts*. Platt was by then the leading British color woodcut artist, after all. Platt wrote the introduction to his book in December 1937. The changes of tone he introduced were similar to the ones that appeared in Brewer's work just two years later.

It would be a mistake to underestimate Brewer. His sense of color was acute, and when it comes to his woodcuts, the reminders of artists as diverse as Oscar Droege, Francis Towne, and John Sell Cotman are all to the good. There is an undoubted touch of Jean Harlow's Hollywood in "Lake Como (The Pergola)." It is not just elegant froth; it's consummate froth. Most British color woodcut artists would have avoided such pale tones to avoid any comparison with watercolor. Even more original is the use of shape in "Mont Blanc." No other color woodcut artist was working in this way, but it is similar to Platt's way of building up images from pieces of tissue laid over each other—one that he taught to his students.

Woodcuts like "Mont Blanc" and "Lake Como (The Pergola)" might have represented Brewer's way of moving away from the etching tradition toward work that appeared to be modern. Collectors of Brewer's etchings may well be bemused by his change of manner, but the fact that he could change and beat other British color woodcut artists at their own game says a good deal about his standards of workmanship. It may not always appeal, but Brewer's professionalism is just as impressive as the distant grandeur of his mountains. John Platt advised would-be color woodcut artists to study the work of great masters like Hokusai and Utamaro. It was to Brewer's credit that he didn't.

Excerpted and adapted with permission from *Modern Printmakers*: https://haji-b.blogspot.com/2017/10/the-colour-woodcuts-of-james-alphege.html.

"Mont Blanc"
(Image courtesy Gavin Smith)

"THE ITALIAN LAKES"

A SERIES OF ORIGINAL ETCHINGS
BY
J. ALPHEGE BREWER

Printed in Colour at one passage through the
press by the Artist

(EDITION LIMITED)

Catalog listings and original labels for Brewer's work suggest that he used a range of intaglio techniques, sometimes in combination, depending on the effect desired. Most labels describe his prints generally as etchings, but a few are more specific. A label for a view of the interior of the York Minster describes it as a drypoint. An exhibition catalog in 1932 lists a view of the Taj Mahal as an aquatint.

Some labels for his color etchings advertise the fact that they were done with a single pass through the press, and this technique may be what Brewer wrote about in his 1916 statement requesting an exemption from serving in WWI (see LIFE STORY). In other words, the "work" Brewer claimed to have "invented" might have been a method for producing the large, dramatic color etchings that were his signature effort and a major source of his income.

At the time, it was not unusual for successful etchers to send their plates out to commercial printers. Brewer's first published etching may have been a "West Front of Ratisbon Cathedral," which was exhibited at the Royal Academy in 1909. Another one, an untitled exterior of Ely Cathedral, was included in a 1911 portfolio of six etchings published by H. R. Howell. This one and in 1912 another,

showing the Portail de la Calende of the cathedral in Rouen, were printed by Charles Welch. But after that, as noted in the December 1915 issue of *The Outlook*, "An interesting thing about Mr. Brewer's colored etchings is that they are printed by himself." As we have seen, "himself" included a staff of as many as eight, including members of the Lucas family, who assisted him in the studio at the back of the family property in Acton.

The idea of printing etchings in color from a single plate had been well documented in an chapter by George W. H. Ritchie in *The Building of a Book* (The Grafton Press, 1906).

> The process, now almost a memory, is a costly one.... This kind of printing requires the plate to be actually painted by hand...and the painting has to be repeated for every impression that is taken....

> The successful printer of color plates must be a rare artist or else work under the direction of an artist. Little of this work is now done except in Paris and Vienna.... Even English plates are usually sent to Paris to be printed.

POSSIBLE CONNECTIONS

While the printing of etchings in color was being done by a number of artists in

France, they usually used a separate plate for each color, *au repérage*. But a few artists painted all the colors on one plate, *à la poupée*. Two artists who were producing engraved color artwork in this way and who might have interacted with Brewer were French-trained American George Senseney and English-born Samuel Arlent Edwards.

Senseney had been teaching the technique in New York for years and had established a reputation for his color etchings *à la poupée*. When Senseney and his wife Dorothy married in London in 1912, Brewer had yet to make any color etchings. It is possible that Brewer learned about the technique at that time from Senseney. His first color etching is dated 1913.

Alternatively, Brewer may have developed his technique for printing color etchings in association with Edwards, who himself claimed to have revived a lost technique for printing color mezzotints from a single plate. The Brewer family lived in the Kensington section of London, and Samuel Edwards attended the nearby Kensington Museum Art School. Did

A 1917 Brewer etching of "Bruges" [Belgium], where S. Arlent Edwards, another artist who printed in color *à la poupée,* lived throughout the duration of WWI.

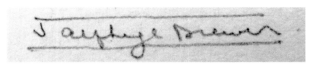

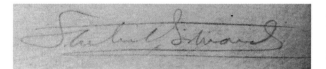

The signatures of J. Alphege Brewer (above) and S. Arlent Edwards (below), both with lines above and below.

Edwards know the children in the artistic Brewer family? James's father was the well-known architectural artist Henry W. Brewer. Samuel and James's older brother Henry were four years apart in age; they might both have been interested in reviving the old, single-plate process for printing color images used before the introduction of modern color lithography. Samuel went off to America in 1890 to pursue this idea, producing best-selling mezzotint copies of famous paintings under the name "S. Arlent Edwards," while Henry might have passed these ideas on to his younger brother James.

In the first years of the 20th century leading up to World War I, Edwards traveled back to England many times and to a second home in Bruges, Belgium. Brewer might have met Edwards or become reacquainted with him at this time. There are large color etchings by Brewer of the cathedral in Brussels and of other scenes elsewhere in Belgium from this period. Edwards and his wife stayed in Bruges throughout the war, and he returned finally to the States only in 1934.

That Brewer had an awareness of Edwards may be apparent in the similarity of their signatures: "J. Alphege Brewer" and "S. Arlent Edwards." I can imagine Brewer thinking that the middle name of Alphege would be just as good as Arlent, perhaps better, as a way of achieving name recognition. Edwards signed his etchings with lines above and below, using an extended cross of the "t" in Arlent (though sometimes unattached) to draw the upper line. I think Brewer improved upon this, using the cap of the "J" to make the upper line, but the similarity between the two signatures is striking.

In 1900, Edwards described what was involved in making his color mezzotints from a single plate, and it is likely that Brewer used some of the same techniques:

Every proof in colors is practically an oil painting. When the plate is engraved and ready to be printed, the colored inks—which are specially ground and mixed with thick oil and varnish—are rubbed on the plate in a thick mass and then wiped off the surface, the fine indentation of the mezzotint leaving a place for the colors to lie. Each color has to be put on and rubbed separately. [To color tiny areas such as the iris of the eye, Edwards would often use a match stick.]

After the ink is put on and the plate wiped and manipulated in a manner which blends the colors together, so that there is no ink left except in the engraved work, the proof-paper is then laid on the plate and is passed through a heavy copper-plate hand-press, the paper being thus pressed into the engraved work in the plate and taking up the ink, and so making the finished proof.

The same process has to be gone over for each proof, and consequently, it necessitates a great amount of labor and experience, but the end justifies the means, for these engravings possess a richness of color which can be achieved by no other process.

WORKING METHODS

The first step for Brewer would have been to limn the image in a wax coating on the surface of a copper plate and then use an acid bath to etch the drawn lines into the plate. Or in some cases, the illustration was inscribed directly, using a drypoint method. (On his etchings, there may have been some extra dry-point work done directly on the plate in order to add character to the lines of the illustration.) Because so many of his early etchings memorialized structures damaged during World War I, it is possible that Brewer used some kind of photographic projection, perhaps with a magic lantern, to mark out the proportions of the buildings and even to aid in reproducing details that had been destroyed.

Then the plate might have been prepared for an aquatint process in order to add some continuous tones for shading. There are etchings that seem to show the addition of aquatint tones in the shadows and others that seem to rely on packed lines and/or cross-hatching.

At this point, Brewer might have produced a monotone "draft" print of the etching, sending it to Alfred Bell & Co. for his publisher to use in proposing a color edition authorized by the Printsellers' Association or Fine Art Trade Guild.

The coloring was not applied afterward in watercolor, nor was the coloring done with a modern three-color process (which would have required three plates, possibly four). Instead, before each impression, all colors were applied directly on the etched plate, probably with a ball-shaped wad of fabric, *à la poupée*. The palette of warm colors for his cathedral etchings could have been mixed by Rembrandt (for example, shades of tawny gold for the main image, reddish orange for roofs, touches of turquoise for water and robes, and perhaps some accent colors for stained glass windows). As Brewer's mid-career sales booklet (see page

Above, a detail from a monotone trial print of Exeter Cathedral, possibly showing the size of a suggested print run.

Some labels for his color etchings advertise the fact that they were done with a single pass through the press, and this technique may be what Brewer wrote about in his 1916 statement requesting an exemption from serving in WWI. In other words, the "work" Brewer claimed to have "invented" might have been an efficient method for producing the large, dramatic color etchings that were his signature effort and a major source of his income.

A comparison of two impressions of the etching "St. Mark's, Venice" (1915), showing the color variations that are an indication that different people may have been involved in "painting" the plates during the print run.

49) said, "...the color schemes are particularly beautiful, giving that feeling of antiquity which is so attractive in this Artist's work." Even with "antiquity" as a goal, the early etchings exhibit at least two distinct color palettes, and these can't be explained by fading or aging. While both palettes must have been acceptable to Brewer, he and his assistants or co-signers must have had different effects in mind. (With changing tastes in the market, and after the Blue Hour series in the early 1920s, his color balance became less "antique" and more natural.)

Part of this inking process might have been to make stencils, allowing the efficient addition of colors to the plate. And while stencils might have guided his assistants in the application of colors—for instance, for the dappled lighting of stained-glass windows—there are other examples where gradations of light blue, rose, and sand are blended to create sky tones. These suggest what one observer called Brewer's "dab hand" at coloring his etchings. There are also etchings where color is applied in a way that would be unlikely if restricted by the use of a stencil (for instance, in the Blue Hour series, where the application of the deep blue may gradually overlap the buildings in the foreground).

In production, the plate would have been inked for the blackish color of the lines of the illustration and the aquatint shadings, then wiped down, leaving the main lines holding ink. After that, stencils could have been used to guide the application of each chosen color until the plate was fully inked for a run through the press. The aquatint toning, if any, would have provided shading for a black-and-white print, and would have darkened tones in the appropriate places when color was applied.

Whether or not the etching had been accepted by the Printsellers' Association or Fine Art Trade Guild, the complete printed edition, titled and signed (and with the tiny copyright inscription at the bottom edge), would have been sent off to Alfred Bell & Co., which supervised the sales and fulfillment operation. For PA/FATG editions, the etchings had to be brought into their office together, along with the plates. They were then all run through their stamping machine in the order in which they were printed and the plates destroyed.

EARLY IMPRESSIONS

There are a number of monotone Brewer etchings in which the etched image does not extend to the edge of the plate, therefore allowing a margin between the impression mark and the image itself. Usually (but not always) this space is used for Brewer's signature and the hand-written title of the etching.

What seems to be the first of these, the massive (19" x 25") "West Front of Ratisbon Cathedral" (at left), his earliest known etching, was exhibited at the Royal Academy in 1909. Two more come from 1911, an untitled exterior of Ely Cathedral printed by Charles Welch as part of the portfolio of six by different artists published by H. R. Howell, and the "Aix La Chapelle (Aachen)" published by Alfred Bell & Co. with an in-plate title (see page 61). Others I've been able to inspect are undated: "Doorway of Church at Wetzler on the Lahn," "The Chancel Ely Cathedral," "The Transepts. York Cathedral," "Sonning on Thames," and "Strand on the Green."

I have not found any similar impressions among his color etchings (which he began making in 1913), nor with any monotone etching that can be dated with certainty after "Aix La Chapelle (Aachen)." An untitled image of the Portail de la Calende in Rouen, published in 1912 by H. R. Howell, comes to the edge of the printing plate, beginning a practice that Brewer seems to have continued throughout his career. It is reasonable to think of the known etchings with a margin (and any others of this kind that are discovered) as among his earliest, probably done between 1909 and 1911, and possibly earlier.

REPRODUCTIONS

Whether or not these Jacobi Re-proofs were authorized by Brewer, their wide circulation must have had a beneficial effect on the scope of the artist's American market.

At least three of Brewer's early images were sold in the United States by Emil Jacobi as "Jacobi Re-proofs." One of these was a reproduction of "The Choir, Norwich Cathedral." Two others portray the exterior and interior of the Cathedral of Notre-Dame in Rheims and are reproductions of etchings that were published in late 1914 at the beginning of World War I. Jacobi may have noticed that a U.S. copyright was not separately claimed on these etchings, a mistake corrected on Brewer's etchings after this. Whether or not these Jacobi Re-proofs were authorized by Brewer, their wide circulation must have had a beneficial effect on the scope of the artist's American market.

While the use of the term "re-proof" suggests a reuse of Brewer's original plates, the label pasted on the back of the exterior view of Rheims Cathedral carefully avoids making this assertion. At the bottom of the label it reads, "This re-proof is a facsimile of a signed proof Color etching.... This Re-Proof retains in a marked degree the subtle technic of the original and bears a facsimile of the artist's signature." (It is not unusual for this part of Jacobi's label to be torn off, indicating that a re-seller might have wanted the buyer to accept both the signature and the art as original.)

The best comparison I've been able to make is between the glorious etching of the rose window at the west end of the cathedral in Rheims and a signed Jacobi Re-proof of the same image. First, at 13.25 x 19 inches, the Jacobi version is almost 15 percent smaller than Brewer's 15.5 x 22.25-inch etching and therefore could not be a re-strike of Brewer's plate. (Also, some Jacobi Re-proofs were published in two different sizes.) The colors follow Brewer's rich hues, with human figures and stained-glass windows in similar tints. The lines of the image are reproduced exactly, down to each cross-hatching mark in the shadows. There is no halftone screen, only an infinitesimal, reticulated pattern not visible to the naked eye. The re-proof carries its own © mark in the bottom right-hand corner, and, tellingly, the tiny U.K. copyright notice of Alfred Bell has been (only partially) obscured. It seems to have been signed in pencil by both Jacobi (lower left) and Brewer (lower right), but as some of the labels for Jacobi Re-proofs admit, Brewer's signature is not claimed to be anything other than a facsimile.

Jacobi described his working method in a chapter of Frederick H. Hitchcock's *The Building of a Book* (The Grafton Press, 1906). He photographed an original artwork to create a contact negative and used this to make a glass, copper, or zinc printing plate with a photo-gelatine process. In this, the areas exposed to

At left: Brewer's original 1914 etching of the rose windows of Rheims Cathedral, published without an American copyright. To its right, Emil Jacobi's "Re-proof" of this etching together with his "Re-proof" of Brewer's 1914 exterior of the west front of Rheims Cathedral.

Top: an item in *The Argus* of Melbourne, Australia, about an exhibition in 1919 featuring works of both Jacobi and Brewer. Below: a poster advertising an exhibition of Jacobi's prints.

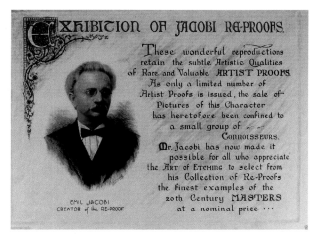

light became hardened raised surfaces capable of holding ink in gradations. Then he colored the plate for each impression (as done with Brewer's color etchings), made the impressions, and signed them in pencil with his own name and a close imitation of the artist's signature.

The success of this process in reprinting artwork was noted by Jacobi: "The depth and richness of tone of an engraving, the delicate tints of an aquarelle or India-ink sketch, and the sharpness of the lines of an etching or pen sketch can be reproduced with such fidelity that it is often impossible to distinguish the copy from the original."

EMIL JACOBI CAREER

Jacobi was born in 1853 in Germany, the son of Carl Heinrich Jacobi, a surveyor for the Royal Westphalian Railway who later became a prize-winning photographer. When Emil was in his early twenties, he ran a printing facility in Golegã, Portugal, which his father co-owned with the aristocrat and photography enthusiast Carlos Relvas. Then his father started the Berlin Phototype Institute, a new company specializing in the "application of photography for the reproduction of oil paintings." "Phototype" was one of the terms used for the photo-gelatine process, examples of which Emil's father had sent to the 1876 Centennial International Exhibition in Philadelphia. When the well-known Philadelphia photographer Frederick Gutekunst negotiated U.S. rights to Jacobi's phototype process, Emil emigrated in 1878 to help set up Gutekunst's printing facility. A year and a half later he was

granted U.S. patent 225,389 for an improvement in the Process of Producing Phototype Plates, which he assigned to Gutekunst, whose printing operation he ran for almost two decades. In the U.S. Census of 1880 and on his naturalization card in 1900, Jacobi was listed as a photographer. In the 1900 census he was living in Brooklyn (where he worked for the Albertype Company) and was identified as "Supt, Photo type" with "pictures" written in above. In the 1910 census, he had moved to Elizabeth, New Jersey, and was listed as "Superintendent, Art Co." (the Campbell Art Company, according to the 1915 city directory for Elizabeth).

At some point, Jacobi advertised an "Exhibition of Jacobi Re-proofs," identifying himself as the "Creator of the Re-proof." At a "nominal price," all "who appreciate the Art of Etching" could select from his collection of "the finest 20th-century masters." These included Axel Herman Haig, Hedley Fitton, Ferdinand Jean Luigini, Maurice Bompard, Fritz Krostewitz, Gaston de Latenay, Andrew F. Affleck, Tavik F. Simon, George Senseney, Frits Thaulow, Fernand Le Goût-Gérard, Edgar L. Pattison, Charles Bartlett, Bruno Bielefeld, Herbert Thomas Dicksee, Anders Zorn, Paul Emile Lecomte, Edward Sharland, Mortimer Menpes, Louis Icart, and Vaughan Trowbridge, among others (including Brewer).

Jacobi died in March 1918, but supplies of Jacobi Re-proofs of the Rheims Cathedral and photolithographic copies of them continued to be sold. After the war, these carried a label describing the war as "late" rather than "present." Similar copies were sold as "Cross

Re-proofs" (with a label very much like the one on the back of Jacobi Re-proofs). Other prints based on these Brewer etchings were sold by the American Art Co., N.Y., Campbell Prints, Inc., N.Y., Buckingham Print, and the Edward Gross Co., Inc., N.Y. The Taber-Prang Art Co. of Springfield, Massachusetts, reproduced these two 1914 images and also sold copies of Brewer's "The Choir, Westminster Abbey" [mislabeled as "The Choir (Westminster Cathedral)"], "Cathedral of St. Gudule, Brussels, Belgium," "Exeter Cathedral," and "The Choir (Norwich Cathedral)," all of them early Brewer etchings published without an American copyright.

A year after Jacobi died, *The Argus* of Melbourne, Australia, announced an exhibition that included his "reproofs" of works by de Latenay, Haig, Fitton, and others. Most interestingly, these were combined with a selection of original etchings by J. Alphege Brewer from the years of the war—the West Front of the Rheims Cathedral, the Cloth Hall in Ypres, and buildings in Verdun, Antwerp, Louvain, Bruges, and elsewhere. This suggests an American source for the exhibition associated with both Jacobi and Brewer—possibly Samuel Schwartz's Sons & Co., which offered "High-Grade Art Reproductions" at their Fifth Avenue gallery. After Jacobi's copies of Brewer's 1914 views of the exterior and interior of Rheims Cathedral had been published, Schwartz's began registering U.S. copyrights in Brewer's name for many original etchings printed in 1915 and 1916, including most of those mentioned in the news item.

It is unknown if Jacobi's reproductions

JACOBI RE-PROOF
Rheims Cathedral (West Front)
After an Original Color Etching by
J. Alphege Brewer

No. 8454—9 x 12 Plate   No 8654—13 x 20 Inch Plate

Work was begun on this cathedral in 1212 under the personal supervision of Archbishop Humbert. He pushed the work with such vigor that it was finished in 1242. The wonderful unity of the architecture attests to the rapidity of the work. The interior is 466 feet long and 121 feet high. The architects were Bernard de Soissons, Gauthier de Reims, Jean d'Orbais and Jean Loops.

At the end of the 13th century the church was enlarged and the structure was completed in the course of the 14th century, from designs of the 13th century, under the architect, Robert de Coucy.

This prodigy of magnificence, with its army of five thousand statues and resplendent windows, which flashed in the rays of the setting sun like a world of sparking jewels, was damaged almost beyond repair during the late war.

The artist of this charming subject, J. Alphege Brewer, was born at Kensington, England, in 1883, and exhibits annually in the Royal Academy, London.

This re-proof is a facsimile of a signed proof Color etching. Color etchings are produced by rubbing the color into the plate, a process that is tedious and requiring great skill. A limited number of copies are pulled from the original plate and signed by the artist. This Re-Proof retains in a marked degree the subtle technic of the original and bears a facsimile of the artist's signature.

The public is cautioned against inferior imitations; genuine Re-Proofs bear the signature

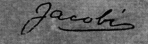

Above: the label for the Jacobi Re-proof of Brewer's 1914 etching "The West Front of Rheims Cathedral." At left: Jacobi's signature in pencil on a published Jacobi Re-proof.

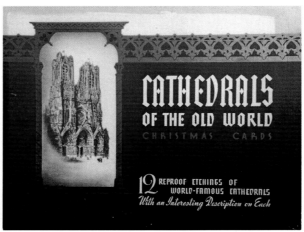

Above: the 1916 Rheims Cathedral image cut as a 352-piece puzzle in the 1930s by Henry A. Martin of Rochester, New York. Top right: the box for a set of Christmas cards, which included an information card, "Color Etchings of Famous Cathedrals by J. Alphege Brewer." At right: a PlaQ-Etching produced in the U.S. in the late 1920s and early 1930s possibly in connection with the fundraising for the cathedral's restoration. It was based on Brewer's 1914 etching.

were authorized by well-known European artists during World War I to maintain sales when shipping across the Atlantic was undependable, or simply to expand their market. It would have been an extra selling point if Jacobi could have said "authorized re-proofs," but he didn't.

BREWER REPURPOSED

The 1914 West Front image was also reproduced as a commemorative plaque in 1929 by the Buckbee-Brehm Co. and by Parker Bros. in 1928 for a 13" x 19" jigsaw puzzle in their Pastime series. (The puzzle seems to be based on the Edward Gross Co. copy.) The 1916 etching of Rheims Cathedral West Front by James and Henry, which did carry an American copyright, was licensed and printed in the late 1920s by the Goes Lithographing Co. in Chicago. These 12" x 16" prints were used by other jigsaw puzzle makers, including Pine Tree Novelty and brothers-in-law Henry A. Martin and Chester W. Nott (a "Nott-Ezy" Puzzle with 500 pieces). Brewer's 1925 West Front version was reproduced in black and white with the copyright notice at the bottom edge cut off, then framed and sold sometime in the 1940s by the Bulfair Art Shop in New York City. In 1948, the Rust Craft card company of Boston issued a collection of Christmas cards titled "Color Etchings of Famous Cathedrals by J. Alphege Brewer," which included, among others, the artist's exterior and interior views of cathedrals in Paris and Rheims, the exterior of the Laon Cathedral, and the interior of St Mark's, Venice.

THE 1925 BROCHURE

A 16-page (cover plus 12-page signature) black-and-white booklet titled "Original Etchings" seems to have been published by Brewer in the middle of 1925. It is a resource for identifying some of his etchings and sorting them by date, and it offers insights into Brewer's artistic approach.

Although the booklet was published without any date or authorship, there are some telltale clues about its provenance. We can assume its date because the most recent datable etchings listed are known to have been published in 1925, but two paired etchings of Rheims Cathedral (the "West Front" and the "Rose Windows from the Chancel"), published in August and September 1925, respectively, were not included (nor any other datable etchings produced in the years after 1925). We can assume it was printed or at least prepared in England because of the spellings of words like "colour" and "recognised." And we know it was aimed at the American market because the prices are in dollars and cents (and because it was found in a shop in upstate New York).

The inside cover lists 20 "Large Etchings Printed in Color," all copyrighted between 1914 and 1921 and published by Alfred Bell & Co. in limited editions authorized by the Printsellers' Association or its successor, the Fine Art Trade Guild. (It is interesting that, for the most part, the etchings described as "not now obtainable in London" in an announcement for a 1919 exhibition of Brewer's etchings in Melbourne, Australia, [see clipping on page 46] are not among the etchings advertised in this booklet.)

After a page of promotional text, the following 10 pages show 29 thumbnail images of FATG-authorized editions mostly published in 1922–25 (but including three earlier etchings listed on the inside cover). Twelve of these etchings are from his Blue Hour series.

On the final inside page of the booklet are pictured six smaller horizontal etchings under the heading "New Five-Fifty Etchings." The booklet introduction on the first page explains: "With a view of bringing his work within the reach of all, his latest enterprises are two series of small etchings, one being printed in Colour and the other drypoints printed in Black and White; doubtless this will add to his already world-wide reputation." The term "five-fifty" presumably refers to a *prix fixe* of $5.50 (ca. $75 today) for these smaller etchings, whether in black and white

*If this isn't J. Alphege Brewer talking about his art,
the quotes are surely sentiments he could have agreed with
and might have either provided or approved.*

or in color. The inside back cover has a complete listing (at that time) of these "five-fifty" etchings, 14 in color and eight in black and white. The color etchings include his little etchings of gates and arches at night, and the black-and-white drypoints include six that document scenes from Venice and also "The Monarch" and "The Lone Pine," both parenthetically described as "Pine Tree Study." None of these were copyrighted by Alfred Bell or imprinted with the FATG stamps, but we can safely date them to 1924–25.

There is a difference between the prices listed in guineas in the FATG archives and the prices in this catalog. The largest color etchings were priced at 8 guineas by Alfred Bell & Co. (which would work out to $375 today), while the $44 cost of similar etchings in this booklet would now be about $600. The difference might be in the markup for a U.S. distributor and include the cost of shipping the etchings overseas.

There is no mention of Alfred Bell & Co. anywhere in the booklet (not even the little "ABC in a bell" logo used in an earlier pamphlet), which is hard to imagine if it had been produced under their auspices. Yet, the publication does not represent any break in the artist's relationship with Alfred Bell & Co., who continued to publish and copyright etchings by Brewer through 1939. A news item in

the April 22, 1928, St. Joseph (MO) *Gazette*—with text lifted from the brochure—says that the American agent for Brewer's "proofs" is Walter E. Iliff of West Orange, New Jersey. In the fall of 1919, Iliff, listed as a salesman in censuses, had traveled to England, and it is possible that arrangements were made then for him to represent the artists published by Alfred Bell & Co. A news item in the March 16, 1920, Richmond (IN) *Palladium* (about a donation of his father's books to his high school library) described Iliff as the American manager for Alfred Bell & Co. An arrangement between Brewer and Samuel Schwartz's Sons in New York City seems to have ended in early 1917, about the time Brewer was called up to serve in the RAF.

In any case, we might guess that the booklet was prepared under Brewer's direction, so that the American market could see which etchings were available from his U.S. distributor. The booklet has markings by hand that indicate with an "X" which etchings were "ALL SOLD." Since a postcard with a 1936 cancellation was found together with the booklet, its use may have continued for a decade after its publication, with updating.

If the booklet was indeed created with the input of J. Alphege Brewer, it provides many insights into the way he regarded himself as an artist. He wears his conservatism as

a badge of honor, writing that "the cult of the ugly has never influenced him" and expressing pleasure in the fact that his work can appeal to the collector while being "understood by the average man." He is proud that the architecture in his etchings "is accurate in every detail" (in part crediting heredity from his father, "the well-known archaeologist" H. W. Brewer), while noting "an underlying softness in his composition." He remembers a favorable second-hand quote from a decade before, when the December 1915 issue of *The Outlook* reported that the *Fine Arts Journal* had said the artist "makes a picture of what in less skillful hands might degenerate into a mere architectural drawing." Stressing that he executes or supervises the printing of the etchings himself, he says that "many of the wonderful effects produced are quite unique and some of the colour schemes are particularly beautiful," catching "all the mystery and romance" of the European cathedrals while giving a "feeling of antiquity." The etchings have atmosphere and light—"'luminosity' in the parlance of the modern art critic"—and combine these characteristics with "a free style and a sane outlook."

If this isn't J. Alphege Brewer talking about his art, the quotes are surely sentiments he could have agreed with and might have either provided or approved.

CATALOG

Artist: JAB=J. Alphege Brewer; HCB=Henry C. Brewer; FSB=F. Sherrin Brewer. Edition=Number of impressions authorized in edition (not necessarily all of them sold). Stamp=Fine Art Trade Guild (FATG) and its predecessor, the Printsellers' Association (PA). Dimensions of image=In inches, horizontal first (some listings may be reversed because of inconsistent source material). Date=Recorded by PA/FATG or otherwise determined. Copyright=Date of copyright when known to be different from PA/FATG listing. Brackets indicate identifying description not in the title. Catalog as of 5/1/21. For updated and corrected entries, visit www.jalphegebrewer.info.

Title	Artist	Edition	Color	Publisher	Cost	Stamp	Dimensions	Date	Copyright
Aix La Chapelle (Aachen)	JAB	150	B&W	Alfred Bell	4gns	PA	13.8 x 20.9	1911	
Aix La Chapelle (trial)	JAB		B&W				13.75 x 20.9	1911	
Amalfi, Italy	JAB	300		Alfred Bell	2gns	FATG	11.5 x 8.5	1932	
Amiens Cathedral	JAB	500	C	Alfred Bell	8gns	PA	18.25 x 25.75	1918	
Amiens Cathedral	JAB	300	B&W	Alfred Bell	4gns	FATG	11.6 x 17.25	1930	1929
Amiens Cathedral (The Nave)	JAB	500	C	Alfred Bell	8gns	PA	18 x 25.5	1919	
Amiens Cathedral (The Nave)	JAB	300	B&W	Alfred Bell	4gns	FATG	11.6 x 17.75	1930	1929
An Old Street in Dieppe	JAB		B&W				7.5 x 9.2	Bef. 1926	
Antwerp	JAB	300	C	Alfred Bell	6gns	PA	21.25 x 16	1915	
Antwerp (An Old Street)	JAB		C				4.75 x 7	Bef. 1926	
Antwerp (Old Meat Market)	JAB		C				4.5 x 7	Bef. 1926	
Antwerp Cathedral [with statue of Rubens]	JAB	300	C	Alfred Bell	6gns	PA	16.75 x 22.75	1917	
Antwerp Harbor (early morning)	JAB	500	C	Alfred Bell	8gns	PA	21.9 x 17.9	1919	
Auxerre, France (Gate of St. Pierre)	JAB		C				4.5 x 7	Bef. 1926	
Balmoral Castle	JAB		C				8.25 x 5.25	Bef. 1926	
Banks of Loch Katrine, The	JAB	300	C	Alfred Bell	2gns	FATG	11 x 9	1939	
Barcelona, Spain	JAB	300		Alfred Bell	2gns	FATG	11.8 x 8.5	1932	
Barnard Castle	JAB		B&W				8.75 x 6.9	Aft. 1925	
Battle Abbey	JAB		B&W				8.9 x 7	Aft. 1925	
Bridge of Sighs, Venice, The [BH]	JAB	300	C	Alfred Bell	6gns	FATG	13.1 x 23.4	1921	
Broadway	JAB		C				7.75 x 6	Aft. 1925	
Bruges (Quai de Rosaire)	JAB	300	C	Alfred Bell	3gns	FATG	6 x 19.75	1939	1938
Bruges (Quai du Rosaire)	JAB	300	C	Alfred Bell	4gns	FATG	10.9 x 16.25	1923	
Bruges [the Belfry]	JAB	300	C	Alfred Bell	4gns	PA	12.9 x 16.1	1917	
Bruges, Pont des Baudets	JAB	300	C	Alfred Bell	2gns	FATG	9.9 x 6.9	1922	
Burgos Cathedral	JAB	200		Alfred Bell	4gns		13.8 x 18.75	Bef. 1915	
Burgos Cathedral [interior]	JAB; HCB	300	C	Alfred Bell	8gns	PA	17.4 x 26.6	1916	
Cambridge (Bridge of Sighs)	JAB	300	B&W	Alfred Bell	2gns	FATG	10 x 7	1921	
Cambridge (Bridge of Sighs)	JAB		B&W				8 x 6	Aft. 1925	
Cambridge (Clare College)	JAB		B&W				8.4 x 5.5	Bef. 1926	
Cambridge (King's College)	JAB		B&W				8.4 x 5.4	Bef. 1926	
Cambridge (King's College Chapel)	JAB	300	B&W	Alfred Bell	2gns	FATG	6.9 x 9.85	1927	
Cambridge (King's and Clare Colleges)	JAB		B&W				9.5 x 4.9	Aft. 1925	

Title	Artist	Edition	Color	Publisher	Cost	Stamp	Dimensions	Date	Copyright
Cambridge (St Johns)	JAB	300	B&W	Alfred Bell	2gns	FATG	6.9 x 10.1	1920	
Cambridge (Trinity College Great Court)	JAB		B&W				8.25 x 5.5	Bef. 1926	
Cambridge (Trinity College Great Court)	JAB		B&W				9.75 x 5	Aft. 1925	
Cambridge (Trinity College)	JAB	300	B&W	Alfred Bell	2gns	FATG	6.9 x 10.1	1920	
Cambridge St. Johns College	JAB	300	B&W	Alfred Bell	2gns	FATG	6.85 x 9.9	1928	
Canterbury	JAB	200	B&W	Alfred Bell	2 gns		7.9 x 11.3	Bef. 1915	
Canterbury (Butchery Lane)	JAB		C				5 x 9.85	Aft. 1925	
Canterbury (Mercery Lane)	JAB		C				5 x 9.85	Aft. 1925	
Canterbury (The Weavers)	JAB		C				4.5 x 7	Bef. 1926	
Canterbury Cathedral	JAB	300	C	Alfred Bell	5gns	PA	12.5 x 18.5	1915	
Canterbury Cathedral [from the south west]	JAB		B&W				8.25 x 5.75	Aft. 1925	
Canterbury Cathedral (from the South West)	JAB	300	B&W	Alfred Bell	4gns	FATG	18 x 11.6	1925	
Castle Combe	JAB		C				8 x 6	Aft. 1925	
Cathedral of St. Gudule, The …, Brussels, Belgium	JAB		C	Alfred Bell			16.75 x 24.2	1914	
Chancel Ely Cathedral, The	JAB		B&W				14.25 x 20.5	Bef. 1913	
Chartres (The Nave)	JAB	300	C	Alfred Bell	4gns	FATG	10.75 x 16.3	1923	
Chester (The East Gate)	JAB		C				6 x 7.6	Aft. 1925	
Chester Cathedral	JAB	300	C	Alfred Bell	3gns	FATG	8 x 14.75	1926	
Chester Cathedral	JAB		C				8.25 x 9.85	Aft. 1925	
Chester Cathedral	JAB		C				6.3 x 8.9	Aft. 1925	
Chester Cathedral	JAB		B&W				6 x 8	Aft. 1925	
Chester Cathedral [chancel looking west]	JAB		C				6 x 7	Aft. 1925	
Choir, Norwich Cathedral, The	JAB	200	B&W	Alfred Bell	6 gns		15.25 x 25	Bef. 1915	
Choir, Westminster Abbey, The	JAB		B&W				15 x 24	Bef. 1915	
Church of Notre Dame, Caudebec, The	JAB							Bef. 1915	
Church of Notre Dame, The..., Dinant-on-the-Meuse,	JAB	300	C	Alfred Bell	6gns	PA	15.5 x 22	1915	
Church of the Holy Sepulchre, Jerusalem	JAB; HCB	500	C	Alfred Bell	6gns	PA	17.1 x 22.6	1918	
Clovelly	JAB		C				4.9 x 9.5	Aft. 1925	
Cockington Forge	JAB		C				7.75 x 5.75	Aft. 1925	
Derwentwater	JAB	300	B&W	Alfred Bell	2gns	FATG	9.9 x 7	1928	
Dieppe	JAB		C	Alfred Bell			14.5 x 12.1	1914	
Dieppe (Church of St. Jacques) [BH]	JAB	300	C	Alfred Bell	2gns	FATG	6 x 11.9	1923	
Doorway of the Church at Wetzlar on the Lahn (trial)	JAB		B&W				8.2 x 13.75	Bef. 1913	
Durham Castle	JAB		C				8.8 x 6.85	Aft. 1925	
Durham Cathedral	JAB	300	B&W	Alfred Bell	2gns	FATG	11.4 x 8.5	1932	
Durham Cathedral	JAB		C				5.5 x 7.5	Aft. 1925	
Durham Cathedral	JAB		B&W				5.75 x 8.25		
Durham Cathedral (The Chancel)	JAB	300	C	Alfred Bell	4gns	FATG	11 x 16.5	1924	
Durham Cathedral (the Nave looking East)	JAB	300	B&W	Alfred Bell	2gns	FATG	8.5 x 11.4	1931	

Title	Artist	Edition	Color	Publisher	Cost	Stamp	Dimensions	Date	Copyright
Durham Cathedral [BH]	JAB	300	C	Alfred Bell	6gns	FATG	13.1 x 23.4	1922	1923
Durham Cathedral, from the Weir	JAB	300		Alfred Bell	2gns	FATG	9.9 x 6.9	1924	
Edinburgh (The Tolbooth)	JAB		C				4.75 x 9.8	Aft. 1925	
Edinburgh Castle	JAB		B&W	Alfred Bell	3gns	FATG	9.8 x 14,5	1927	
Edinburgh, John Knox's House	JAB	400	B&W	Alfred Bell	3gns	FATG	10 x 14.6	1926	
Edinburgh (John Knox's House)	JAB		C				4.75 x 9.8	Aft. 1925	
Edinburgh (St. Giles Cathedral)	JAB	300	B&W	Alfred Bell	3gns	FATG	8 x 15.1	1925	1924
Ely Cathedral	JAB		B&W				5.75 x 8.25	Aft. 1925	
Ely Cathedral [exterior, untitled]	JAB	400	B&W	H.R. Howell			12.8 x 18.75	1911	
Ely Cathedral, from the South-West	JAB	300	B&W	Alfred Bell	2gns	FATG	9.9 x 6.9	1924	
Eros	JAB		C				6 x 8	Aft. 1925	
Evening on the Meuse. Huy.	JAB; FSB	300	C	Alfred Bell	6gns	PA	22.9 x 16	1916	
Exeter Cathedral (The West Front)	JAB	300	B&W	Alfred Bell	2gns	FATG	11.4 x 8.5	1930	
Exeter Cathedral [interior]	JAB	[150]	C				14.4 x 20.5	Bef. 1926	
Exeter Cathedral, South Tower [BH]	JAB	300	C	Alfred Bell	3gns	FATG	7.9 x 15.1	1922	1923
Gloucester (College Court)	JAB		C				4.9 x 9.9	Bef. 1926	
Gloucester (the New Inn)	JAB		C				8.25 x 5.25	Bef. 1926	
Gloucester Cathedral [The Great East Window]	JAB	300	B&W	Alfred Bell	3gns	FATG	8 x 15	1925	1924
Granada from the Albacyn	JAB; HCB	300	C	Alfred Bell	6gns	PA	22.75 x 16.1	1917	
Groot Constantia	JAB		C				10 x 6.7	Aft. 1925	
Head of Loch Lomond	JAB	300		Alfred Bell	2gns	FATG	6 x 11.9	1926	
Horse Guards (London), The	JAB		C				7.8 x 5.8	Aft. 1925	
Hotel de Ville, Arras	JAB	300	C	Alfred Bell	6gns	PA	16.1 x 21.9	1917	
Hotel de Ville, Louvain	JAB	300	C	Alfred Bell	5gns	PA	13.1 x 18.9	1915	
Into the Light	JAB	300	C	Alfred Bell	4gns	FATG	11 x 16.4	1933	
Isle of Arran (Glen Sannox)	JAB		C				8.25 x 5.5	Bef. 1926	
La Rue de la Grosse Horloge, Rouen [BH]	JAB	300	C	Alfred Bell	3gns	FATG	7.9 x 15	1922	1923
Lake Como (Gravedona)	JAB		C				7.75 x 5.75	Aft. 1925	
Lake Como (Azzano)	JAB	300	C	Alfred Bell	3gns	FATG	6 x 19.75	1939	1938
Lake Como (Balbianello)	JAB		C				4.8 x 9.4	Aft. 1925	
Lake Como (Bellagio)	JAB	300	C	Alfred Bell	2gns	FATG	5 x 15	1933	
Lake Como (Menaggio)	JAB	300	C	Alfred Bell	2gns	FATG	9.9 x 6.9	1925	
Lake Como (Near Bellagio)	JAB	300	C	Alfred Bell	2gns	FATG	6 x 11.9	1930	
Lake Como (Varenna)	JAB	300	C	Alfred Bell	2gns	FATG	6 x 11.9	1930	
Lake Como, from the Villa Carlotta	JAB	300	C	Alfred Bell	6gns	FATG	23.4 x 14.1	1926	
Lake Geneva	JAB	300		Alfred Bell	2gns	FATG	11.5 x 8.5	1935	
Lake Lugano (Gandria)	JAB	300	C	Alfred Bell	2gns	FATG	5 x 15	1933	
Lake Lugano (Lugano)	JAB	300	C	Alfred Bell	2gns	FATG	9.9 x 6.9	1925	
Lake Lugano (Morcote)	JAB	300	C	Alfred Bell	3gns	FATG	6.1 x 19.75	1926	

Title	Artist	Edition	Color	Publisher	Cost	Stamp	Dimensions	Date	Copyright
Lake Lugano (Oria)	JAB		C				4.8 x 9.4	Aft. 1925	
Lake Maggiore (Isola Bella)	JAB		C				7.75 x 5.75	Aft. 1925	
Laon Cathedral	JAB; HCB	300	C	Alfred Bell	6gns	PA	16.9 x 24	1917	
Lincoln Cathedral	JAB		C				7.25 x 9.5	Aft. 1925	
Lincoln Cathedral	JAB		B&W				5.9 x 7.9	Bef. 1926	
Liverpool Cathedral (Choir looking East)	JAB	300	C	Alfred Bell	4gns	FATG	11 x 16.5	1924	
Liverpool Cathedral (The Choir)	JAB	400	C	Alfred Bell	2gns	FATG	8.4 x 11.4	1933	
Liverpool Cathedral, The Lady Chapel	JAB	300	B&W	Alfred Bell	3gns	FATG	7.9 x 15	1924	
Loch Katrine (& Ellen's Isle)	JAB		C				7.25 x 5.4	Bef. 1926	
Loch Lomond	JAB		C				7.75 x 5.75	Aft. 1925	
Loch Lomond (and Ben Lomond)	JAB	300	C	Alfred Bell	2gns	FATG	12 x 9	1939	
Loch Lomond (From Tarbet)	JAB		C				8.25 x 5.3	Bef. 1926	
Loches, France (Hotel de Ville)	JAB	300		Alfred Bell	3gns	FATG	8 x 15.1	1923	
Louvain (St. Gertrude)	JAB	300	C	Alfred Bell	6gns	PA	17.5 x 21.25	1915	
Louvain (the Church of St. Gertrude)	JAB	325	C	Alfred Bell	6gns	FATG	17 x 21.9	1921	
Malines	JAB	300	C	Alfred Bell	5gns	PA	12.9 x 18.4	1915	
Malines (from the Rue de Beffer)	JAB		C				4.5 x 7	Bef. 1926	
Malines, Notre Dame d'Hauswych	JAB	300	C	Alfred Bell	2gns	FATG	9.9 x 6.9	1922	
Matterhorn (from Zermatt)	JAB	300		Alfred Bell	2gns	FATG	8.5 x 11.5	1935	
Milan Cathedral (Corso V Emanuele)	JAB	300	B&W	Alfred Bell	4gns	FATG	11.8 x 17.9	1927	
Milan Cathedral (The Nave looking East)	JAB	200		Alfred Bell	4gns	FATG	11.6 x 17.9	1925	
Milan Cathedral (The West Front)	JAB	200	B&W	Alfred Bell	4gns	FATG	11.6 x 17.6	1925	
Namur (Church of St. Jean-Baptiste) [BH]	JAB	300	C	Alfred Bell	2gns	FATG	6 x 11.9	1923	
Nave looking East, Rheims Cathedral	JAB	300	C	Alfred Bell	6gns	PA	15.75 x 22.6	1915	1916
North Transept, Rheims Cathedral, The	JAB	300	C	Alfred Bell	6gns	PA	13.9 x 23.75	1918	
Norwich Cathedral	JAB		B&W	Alfred Bell	6gns		5.9 x 8.25	Aft. 1925	
Notre Dame, Paris	JAB; HCB	300	C	Alfred Bell	6gns	PA	15.4 x 22.25	1919	
Notre Dame, Paris (The North Transept)	JAB	300	C	Alfred Bell	6gns	FATG	14.25 x 22.25	1927	
Notre Dame. Paris.	JAB	300	C	Alfred Bell	6gns	FATG	14.25 x 22	1927	
Octogen Ely Cathedral, The	JAB	150	B&W	Alfred Bell	4gns	PA	13.75 x 21	1912	
Old Curiosity Shop, The	JAB		C				7.9 x 6	Aft. 1925	
Old Houses, Holborn	JAB		C				7.75 x 5.9	Aft. 1925	
On the Canal [Sambre], Old Namur	JAB		C	H. R. Howell			15.5 x 10.25	1914	
Oxford (Brasenose College & High Street)	JAB	300	C	Alfred Bell	3gns	FATG	13.6 x 8.9	1921	
Oxford (Christ Church)	JAB	300	B&W	Alfred Bell	2gns	FATG	6 x 11.5	1922	
Oxford, Christ Church	JAB	300	B&W	Alfred Bell	2gns	FATG	6.8 x 9.8	1927	
Oxford (Christchurch College and Cathedral)	JAB	300		Alfred Bell	3gns	FATG	13.4 x 9	1931	
Oxford (High Street)	JAB	300	B&W	Alfred Bell	2gns	FATG	11.4 x 8.4	1929	
Oxford (Magdalen College)	JAB		B&W				8 x 5.4	Bef. 1926	

Title	Artist	Edition	Color	Publisher	Cost	Stamp	Dimensions	Date	Copyright
Oxford (Merton College)	JAB		B&W				8.25 x 5.25	Bef. 1926	
Oxford (Oriel College and St. Mary's Church)	JAB	300	B&W	Alfred Bell	2gns	FATG	6 x 11.9	1922	
Oxford (Oriel College)	JAB		B&W				8.4 x 5.2	Bef. 1926	
Oxford (The Turl and Lincoln College)	JAB	300		Alfred Bell	2gns	FATG	6 x 11.9	1931	
Oxford, Magdalen from the Cherwell [BH]	JAB	300	C	Alfred Bell	3gns	FATG	7.9 x 15.1	1922	
Palais de Justice from the Boulevard Waterloo, Brussels	JAB	300	C	Alfred Bell	5gns	PA	12.9 x 18.4	1915	
Pass of Killiecrankie, The	JAB	300	B&W	Alfred Bell	2gns	FATG	6 x 11.9	1926	
Peter Pan [Kensington Gardens]	JAB		C					Aft. 1925	
Peterborough Cathedral	JAB		B&W				5.75 x 8.25	Aft. 1925	
Porlock	JAB		C				7.9 x 5.9	Aft. 1925	
Ratisbon on the Danube	JAB		C	Alfred Bell			15 x 12.5	1913	
Rheims (The Rose Windows from the Chancel)	JAB	500	C	Alfred Bell	4gns	FATG	10.9 x 16.25	1925	
Rheims Cathedral (The Rose Windows)	JAB	400		Alfred Bell	2gns	FATG	8.4 x 11.4	1932	
Rheims Cathedral (the West Front)	JAB	500	C	Alfred Bell	8gns	FATG	18.1 x 25.75	1921	
Rheims Cathedral (the west front)	JAB	500	C	Alfred Bell	4gns	FATG	10.8 x 16.4	1925	
Rheims Cathedral (West Front)	JAB	400	C	Alfred Bell	2gns	FATG	8.4 x 11.4	1931	1932
Rheims Cathedral [exterior]	JAB; HCB	500	C	Alfred Bell	6gns	PA	16.75 x 23.25	1915	1916
Rheims Cathedral [exterior]	JAB		C	Alfred Bell			15.25 x 21.75	1919	
Rheims Cathedral [exterior]	JAB	300	C	Alfred Bell	6gns	FATG	14.5 x 22.25	1928	
Rheims Cathedral from the South West	JAB	500	C	Alfred Bell	6gns	PA	23.8 x 19.5	1917	
Rheims Cathedral, The West Front of	JAB		C	Alfred Bell			15 x 22.9	1914	
Rheims, The Rose Windows from the Nave	JAB	300	C	Alfred Bell	3gns	FATG	7.9 x 15	1924	
Rome (The Vatican Library)	JAB	300		Alfred Bell	2gns	FATG	11.4 x 8.4	1932	
Rose Windows, Rheims Cathedral, The	JAB		C	Alfred Bell			15.5 x 22.25	1914	
Rose Windows, Rheims Cathedral, The	JAB	300	C	Alfred Bell	8gns	PA	18.25 x 25.75	1915	1916
Rose Windows, Rheims Cathedral, The	JAB		C	Alfred Bell			15.35 x 22.24	1919	
Rouen (The Church of St. Maclou)	JAB	300	B&W	Alfred Bell	4gns	FATG	11.8 x 18	1929	
Rouen (The Portail de la Calende)	JAB	300	B&W	Alfred Bell	4gns	FATG	11.8 x 17.9	1927	
Rouen [The Portail de la Calende]	JAB		B&W	H. R. Howell			11.8 x 19.7	1912	
Rouen Cathedral from the East (trial)	JAB		B&W				14.25 x 19.75	Bef. 1914	
Rouen Cathedral from the East [BH]	JAB	300	C	Alfred Bell	3gns	FATG	8 x 15.1	1922	
Rue de L'ane Aveugle, Bruges [BH]	JAB	300	C	Alfred Bell	3gns	FATG	7.9 x 15.1	1921	
Rue du Bac, Rouen [BH]	JAB	300	C	Alfred Bell	3gns	FATG	7.9 x 15.25	1921	
Rydal Water	JAB	300		Alfred Bell	2gns	FATG	10 x 7	1928	
Salisbury (High Street Gate) [BH]	JAB	300	C	Alfred Bell	3gns	FATG	7.9 x 14.9	1922	
Salisbury Cathedral	JAB		B&W	Alfred Bell	2gns	FATG	6.8 x 9.75	1927	
Seville Cathedral	JAB	300	C	Alfred Bell	6gns	FATG	14.2 x 22.25	1927	
Sonning on Thames	JAB		B&W				8.5 x 5.7	Bef. 1913	
Sorrento (Italy)	JAB	300	C	Alfred Bell	3gns	FATG	6.1 x 19.75	1926	

Title	Artist	Edition	Color	Publisher	Cost	Stamp	Dimensions	Date	Copyright
South Transept Westminster Abbey, The	JAB	500	C	Alfred Bell	8gns	PA	16.5 x 26	1920	
South Transept, Rheims Cathedral, The	JAB	500	C	Alfred Bell	6gns	PA	13.9 x 23.75	1919	
Southampton West Gate	JAB		C				4.5 x 7	Bef. 1926	
Spain (a court in the Generalife)	JAB	300	C	Alfred Bell	3gns	FATG	13.75 x 8.9	1927	
St. Ives (Barnoon Hill)	JAB		C				4.8 x 9.9	Aft. 1925	
St. Mark's, Venice	JAB; HCB	300	C	Alfred Bell	6gns	PA	17.5 x 22.25	1915	
St. Mark's, Venice [exterior]	JAB; HCB	500	C	Alfred Bell	6gns	PA	21.9 x 15.75	1920	
St. Michael's Mount	JAB		C				7.75 x 6	Aft. 1925	
St. Paul's (From Bank Side)	JAB		C				7.75 x 5.75	Aft. 1925	
St. Paul's Cathedral (From Bank Side)	JAB	300	C	Alfred Bell	3gns	FATG	7.75 x 14.75	1927	
St. Paul's Cathedral (From Fleet Street)	JAB	300	C	Alfred Bell	4gns	FATG	10.75 x 16.25	1934	
St. Paul's Cathedral (The Chancel)	JAB	500	C	Alfred Bell	8gns	PA	16.5 x 26	1920	
St. Paul's Cathedral (The Chancel)	JAB	300	C	Alfred Bell	3gns	FATG	9.75 x 14.2	1932	
St. Paul's Cathedral (The Incoming Tide)	JAB	300	C	Alfred Bell	8gns	FATG	23.75 x 16.75	1929	
St. Paul's Cathedral (The Nave)	JAB	200		Alfred Bell	2gns	FATG	8.5 x 11.5	1934	
St. Paul's Cathedral from Fleet Street	JAB		C	Alfred Bell	6gns	FATG	14.9 x 21.4	1926	
St. Paul's Cathedral, from Ludgate Hill [BH]	JAB	300	C	Alfred Bell	3gns	FATG	8 x 14.75	1923	
St. Paul's from the Thames [early morning]	JAB	500	C	Alfred Bell	8gns	PA	24.25 x 16.9	1920	
St. Pauls Cathedral (from Bank-Side)	JAB		C				8.2 x 5.3	Bef. 1926	
Staircase in St. Maclou, Rouen	JAB	300	C	Alfred Bell	3gns	PA	7.25 x 13.4	1915	
Strand on the Green	JAB		B&W				8.5 x 5.75	Bef. 1913	
Street in Cordoba, A	JAB	300	B&W	Alfred Bell	2gns	FATG	5.85 x 11.9	1927	
Street in Seville, A	JAB	300	B&W	Alfred Bell	2gns	FATG	6 x 11.9	1927	
Street in Seville, A	JAB; HCB	300	C	Alfred Bell	6gns	PA	14.9 x 23.5	1916	
Street in Toledo, A	JAB	300	B&W	Alfred Bell	2gns	FATG	6 x 11.9	1927	
Taj Mahal (India), The	JAB	300	C	Alfred Bell	3gns	FATG	13.6 x 8.9	1926	
The Lone Pine	JAB		B&W				4.4 x 9.9	Bef. 1926	
The Monarch	JAB		B&W				4.5 x 10	Bef. 1926	
Thomas Hardy's Birthplace	JAB		C				7.8 x 5.8	Aft. 1925	
Toledo Cathedral	JAB; HCB	300	C	Alfred Bell	8gns	PA	17.75 x 26.9	1918	
Tongres, Belgium (the Old Town Gate)	JAB		C				4.75 x7	Bef. 1926	
Tower Bridge, London, The	JAB		C				8.2 x 5.25	Bef. 1926	
Tower Bridge, The	JAB		C				7.75 x 5.75	Aft. 1925	
Transept, Seville Cathedral, The	JAB; HCB	300	C	Alfred Bell	8gns	PA	17.75 x 26.75	1916	
Transepts. York Cathedral.,The	JAB		B&W				13.5 x 21	Bef. 1913	
Tras-coro Burgos Cathedral, The	JAB; HCB	500	C	Alfred Bell	8gns	PA	17.75 x 26.75	1919	
Trinity College (Cambridge)	JAB	300	B&W	Alfred Bell	2gns	FATG	6.8 x 9.75	1928	
Vatican Library, Rome	JAB			Alfred Bell				1932	
Venice	JAB		B&W				12.5 x 5	Aft. 1925	

Title	Artist	Edition	Color	Publisher	Cost	Stamp	Dimensions	Date	Copyright
Venice (Palazzo Ca D'Oro)	JAB	300	B&W	Alfred Bell	3gns	FATG	14.9 x 9.9	1929	
Venice (San Giorgio)	JAB		B&W				12 x 5	Aft. 1925	
Venice (Santa Maria della Salute)	JAB		B&W				12 x 5	Aft. 1925	
Venice (St. Mark's)	JAB		B&W				8.25 x 5.25	Bef. 1926	
Venice (The Bridge of Sighs)	JAB	200	B&W/C	Alfred Bell	3gns	FATG	8.9 x 13.5	1931	
Venice (The Bridge of Sighs)	JAB		B&W				4.9 x 8.5	Bef. 1926	
Venice (the Bridge of the Rialto)	JAB		B&W				8.2 x 5.2	Bef. 1926	
Venice (The Doge's Palace)	JAB		B&W				8.25 x 5.25	Bef. 1926	
Venice (The Grand Canal)	JAB	500	C	Alfred Bell	4gns	FATG	16.6 x 10.6	1921	
Venice (The Grand Canal)	JAB		B&W				8.25 x 5.2	Bef. 1926	
Venice [the Doge's Palace]	JAB	300	C	Alfred Bell	6gns	PA	23.5 x 15	1916	
Venice, Rio del Greci	JAB		B&W				4.9 x 8.75	Bef. 1926	
Venice, St Marks [interior]	JAB	300		Alfred Bell	6gns	FATG	14.5 x 22.5	1932	
Venice, the Bridge of the Rialto	JAB	200		Alfred Bell	3gns	FATG	13.5 x 8.9	1932	
Venice, the Bridge of the Rialto [BH]	JAB	300	C	Alfred Bell	6gns	FATG	23.4 x 14.1	1922	
Venice, The Doges Palace [BH]	JAB	300	C	Alfred Bell	6gns	FATG	23.4 x 13.9	1923	
Verdun from the Meuse	JAB	300	C	Alfred Bell	5gns	PA	19.5 x 13.25	1916	
Verona (Via S. Maria Antica)	JAB	300		Alfred Bell	2gns	FATG	6 x 11.9	1931	
West Front of Ratisbon Cathedral	JAB	100?	B&W				19 x 25	1909	
Westminster	JAB		C				7.75 x 6	Aft. 1925	
Westminster - Houses of Parliament	JAB	300	C	Alfred Bell	2gns	PA	12 x 8	1918	
Westminster - Houses of Parliament (from the River)	JAB		C				8.25 x 5.25	Bef. 1926	
Westminster (Big Ben)	JAB	300	C	Alfred Bell	3gns	FATG	8 x 14.9	1923	
Westminster (Boats Moving off)	JAB	300		Alfred Bell	8gns	FATG	23.75 x 17	1929	
Westminster Abbey (The Chancel)	JAB	300	B&W	Alfred Bell	3gns	FATG	8 x 15	1929	1928
Westminster Abbey (The West Front)	JAB	300		Alfred Bell	3gns	FATG	9.9 x 14.4	1937	
Westminster Abbey (with Coronation Chair)	JAB	300	C	Alfred Bell	3gns	FATG	9.75 x 14.25	1937	
Westminster Exterior	JAB: HCB		C	Alfred Bell			24.25 x 17	1920	
Where Shakespeare Sleeps (Stratford-on-Avon)	JAB; HCB	500	C	Alfred Bell	6gns	FATG	15.25 x 21.75	1921	
Windsor (St. Georges Chapel, The Choir)	JAB	300		Alfred Bell	2gns	FATG	8.5 x 11.4	1931	
Windsor (St. Georges Chapel)	JAB	300	C	Alfred Bell	4gns	FATG	10.75 x 16.25	1931	1930
Windsor Castle	JAB	500	C	Alfred Bell	5gns	PA	19.25 x 12.4	1919	
York (Bootham Bar)	JAB		C				9 x 7	Aft. 1925	
York (Bootham Bar)	JAB		B&W				5.3x 10.9	Aft. 1925	
York (Bootham Bar)	JAB		C				8.5 x 5.1	Bef. 1926	
York (Monk Bar)	JAB		B&W				5.5 x 9.5	Aft. 1925	
York (Petergate)	JAB		C				4.75 x 9.9	Aft. 1925	
York (Petergate)	JAB		B&W				5 x 8.6	Bef. 1926	
York (St. Williams College)	JAB		B&W				8.8 x 6.9	Aft. 1925	

Title	Artist	Edition	Color	Publisher	Cost	Stamp	Dimensions	Date	Copyright
York (The Shambles)	JAB		B&W				5 x 8.75	Aft. 1925	
York (The Shambles)	JAB		C				5 x 9	Bef. 1926	
York Minster	JAB		B&W				5.9 x 7.9	Aft. 1925	
York Minster	JAB		B&W				7.75 x 5.75	Aft. 1925	
York Minster (The East Window)	JAB		B&W				4.75 x 9.9	Aft. 1925	
York Minster (The Five Sisters Window)	JAB	300	B&W	Alfred Bell	3gns	FATG	7.75 x 14.75	1924	
York Minster (The Five Sisters Window)	JAB	500	C	Alfred Bell	4gns	FATG	11 x 16.5	1926	
York Minster (The Five Sisters Window)	JAB		B&W				4.9 x 9.75	Bef. 1926	
York Minster (The Great East Window)	JAB	300	C	Alfred Bell	3gns	FATG	8 x 15.1	1924	
York Minster (the Oak Leaf Window)	JAB		B&W				5 x 10	Aft. 1925	
York Minster (The Transepts)	JAB	300	B&W	Alfred Bell	3gns	FATG	8 x 14.8	1927	
York Minster [West Front]	JAB			Alfred Bell				1931	
York Minster [West Front]	JAB		C				4.8 x 8.8	Bef. 1926	
York Minster from the East	JAB		B&W	Alfred Bell		FATG	11.4 x 17.5	1924	
York Minster from the East	JAB	400		Alfred Bell	2gns	FATG	8.4 x 11.4	1933	
York Minster from the East	JAB		C				4.9 x 9.9	Aft. 1925	
York Minster from the East	JAB		C				6.5 x 12.5	Aft. 1925	
York Minster from the South West	JAB	300		Alfred Bell	4gns	FATG	17.9 x 11.6	1926	
York Minster from the South West	JAB	300		Alfred Bell	8gns	FATG	22.25 x 17.25	1929	
York Minster, The Crossing	JAB	300	C	Alfred Bell	8gns	FATG	23.5 x 17.9	1929	
York Minster, the Five Sisters Window	JAB	400		Alfred Bell	2gns	FATG	6.4 x 12.9	1932	
York, Bootham Bar [BH]	JAB	300	C	Alfred Bell	3gns	FATG	8 x 14.9	1923	
York, Petergate [BH]	JAB	300	C	Alfred Bell	3gns	FATG	7.9 x 15.1	1922	
Ypes Cathedral	JAB		B&W	Alfred Bell			5.9 x 11.75	1930	
Ypres [Cloth Hall]	JAB	300	C	Alfred Bell	6gns	PA	17 x 21.9	1915	
Ypres [Cloth Hall]	JAB; FSB	300	C	Alfred Bell	6gns	PA	22.9 x 15.75	1918	

ENDNOTES

LIFE STORY

9 Henry W. Brewer: "Up, Up, and Away over Westminster," Carlton Hobbs LLC, last modified September 17, 2015, http://www.carltonhobbs.net/news/up-up-and-away-over-westminster/2015/09/17/.

9 John Sherren Brewer, Jr.: "John Sherren Brewer," Wikipedia, last modified January 1, 2021, https://en.wikipedia.org/w/index.php?title=John_Sherren_Brewer&oldid=997586636.

9 E. Cobham Brewer: "E. Cobham Brewer," Wikipedia, last modified April 27, 2021, https://en.wikipedia.org/w/index.php?title=E._Cobham_Brewer&oldid=1020185060.

9 Henry C. Brewer: "Henry Charles Brewer," Wikipedia, last modified February 16, 2020, https://en.wikipedia.org/wiki/Henry_Charles_Brewer.

9 David Lucas: Victorian Art History, "David Lucas (1802-1881)," All Things Victorian, accessed May 25, 2021, http://www.avictorian.com/Lucas_David.html.

9–10 a statement in support of his request for exemption: "Case Number: M2693," The National Archive, accessed May 25, 2021, http://discovery.nationalarchives.gov.uk/details/r/C14092675.

10 $300,000 in today's dollars: "Historical Currency Conversions," accessed July 29, 2021, https://futureboy.us/fsp/dollar.fsp?quantity=3000&currency=pounds&fromYear=1916.

11 the Royal Cambrian Academy (RCA): "Plas Mawr Catalogues," Royal Cambrian Academy Crown, accessed May 25, 2021, http://rcaconwy.org/about/archive-documents.

11 the Society of Graphic Art: John Carpenter, "Works by James Alphege Brewer exhibited at the Society of Graphic Art, London," JAlphegeBrewer.info, accessed May 25, 2021, https://www.jalphegebrewer.info/sga-listed-works.

11 the Ealing Arts Club: "Ealing Art Group Archives," Ealing Art Group, accessed May 25, 2021, http://www.ealingartgroup.moonfruit.com/archives/4587391519.

11 the December 1915 issue of the New York political magazine: "Architectural Sacrifices of the Great European War," The Outlook (New York), December 8, 1915, 836–37.

12 represent the swan song of British interest in making woodcuts: Gordon Clarke, "The colour woodcuts of James Alphege Brewer," Modern Printmakers, last modified October 21, 2017, https://haji-b.blogspot.com/2017/10/the-colour-woodcuts-of-james-alphege.html.

12 the nickname "Major": Phone call with Brewer's nephew Tom Lynch. February 28, 2018.

ETCHINGS OVERVIEW

14 the master of them all: "Etchings from Warring Europe," *Cincinnati Enquirer* (Cincinnati, Ohio), March 21 1915, 59.

15 the Dubois bronze statue of Joan of Arc: "Joan of Arc (Dubois)," Wikipedia, last modified February 21, 2021, https://en.wikipedia.org/w/index.php?title=Joan_of_Arc_(Dubois)&oldid=1008175169.

EARLY ART

18 *The Girl's Own Paper*: "The Girl's Own Paper," Wikipedia, last modified March 2, 2021, https://en.wikipedia.org/w/index.php?title=The_Girl%27s_Own_Paper&oldid=1009850155.

18 members of the Brewer family were involved: See Brewer articles at Moira Allen, "Victorian Voices," https://www.victorianvoices.net/index.shtml.

20 As one observer has noted: Email to author from collector Gavin Smith.

WARTIME ETCHINGS

21 These etchings were made shortly before the war: "Architectural Sacrifices of the Great European War," *The Outlook* (New York), December 8, 1915, 836–37.

21 the Schlieffen Plan (even with Moltke's adjustments): Barbara W. Tuckman, *The Guns of August,* The Macmillan Company, New York, 1962, 25.

21 the holdings of the museum of the Royal United Service Institution: "Secretary's Notes," *Journal of the United Service Institution*, Vol. 63 (1918): xvi–xvii.

25 the secretary to the U.S. legation in Brussels wrote: Hugh Gibson, "A Journal from Our Legation in Belgium," Project Gutenberg, last modified August 1, 2006, https://www.gutenberg.org/files/18959/18959-h/18959-h.htm#september_1914.

28 issued a proclamation that included: "Edmund Allenby, 1st Viscount Allenby," Wikipedia, last modified May 9, 2021, https://en.wikipedia.org/w/index.php?title=Edmund_Allenby,_1st_Viscount_Allenby&oldid=1022291423.

29 as noted by Alan Kramer: Alan Kramer, *Dynamic of Destruction: Culture and Mass Killing in the First World War,* Oxford University Press, London, 2007, 55.

WARTIME ETCHINGS CONTEXT

30 In a 2014 article in *The Guardian*: Margaret MacMillan, "Did artists foresee the first world war?," *The Guardian,* last modified March 27, 2014, https://www.theguardian.com/artanddesign/2014/mar/27/did-art-foresee-first-world-war.

30 as Marc Swed has written: Marc Swed, "Schoenberg knew. When the world goes mad, send in the clowns," *The Los Angeles Times,* last modified November 25, 2020, https://www.latimes.com/entertainment-arts/story/2020-11-25/how-to-listen-classical-music-schoenberg-pierrot-lunaire.

30 Alan Kramer thought Meidner's visions: Kramer, *Dynamic of Destruction: Culture and Mass Killing in the First World War,* 174.

31 Sophie Goetzmann, however, sounded a cautionary note: Sophie Goetzmann, "Meidner's Urban Iconography: Optical Destruction and Visual Apocalypse," in: Marco Folin and Monica Preti (ed.), *Wounded Cities: The Representation of Urban Disasters in European Art* (14th-20th Centuries), Brill, Leiden, 2015.

31 Jay Winter, in *Sites of Memory, Sites of Mourning*, agreed: Jay Winter, *Sites of Memory, Sites of Mourning,* Cambridge University Press, Cambridge, 2014, 158.

32 They could go anywhere they wanted to go: Alfred Emile Cornebise, *Art from the Trenches: America's Uniformed Artists in World War I,* Texas A&M University Press, College Station, 1991.

33 ill-judged in their appeal: T. Milliingworth, "George Bellows 'War Series'," Fmpinspiriation, last modified April 30, 2014, https://fmpinspiration.wordpress.com/2014/04/30/george-bellows-war-series/.

33 etching revival: Martha Tedeschi, in "The New Language of Etching in Nineteenth-Century England" in: *The Writing of Modern Life: The Etching Revival in France, Britain, and the U.S., 1850–1940*, Smart Museum of Art, Chicago, 26.

33 a sonnet by American poet Hortense Flexner: "Hortense Flexner," Wikipedia, last modified April 28, 2021, https://en.wikipedia.org/wiki/Hortense_Flexner.

33 What Abbé Morel said of the *Miserere* series: Winter, *Sites of Memory, Sites of Mourning,* 174.

A PERSONAL REVELATION

35 Raymond A. Moody, Jr., M.D., writes of the near-death experience: Raymond A. Moody Jr, *Life After Life*, Bantam Books, New York, 1975, 58.

WOODCUTS

37 Perhaps Brewer knew the work of John Platt and his book, *Colour Woodcuts*: John Edgar Platt, *Colour woodcuts: A book of reproductions and a handbook of method*, Sir I. Pitman & Sons, London, 1938.

TECHNIQUES

38 intaglio techniques: "Printmaking Techniques, Defined and Explained in Plain English," accessed May 25, 2021, https://news.masterworksfineart.com/2021/01/20/printmaking-techniques-defined-and-explained-in-plain-english#3-intaglio.

38 An interesting thing about Mr. Brewer's colored etchings: "Architectural Sacrifices of the Great European War," *The Outlook* (New York), December 8, 1915, 836–37.

38 printing etchings in color from a single plate: George W. H. Ritchie, "Printing Intaglio Plates," in: Frederick H. Hitchcock (ed.), *The Building of a Book: A Series of Practical Articles,* The Grafton Press, New York, 1906, 196.

39 French-trained American George Senseney: Erik Senseney and James Mellor, "George Eyster Senseney: Pioneer of American Color Painting," georgesenseney.com, accessed May 25, 2021, http://georgesenseney.com/hindex.html.

39 established a reputation for his color etchings *à la poupée*: The WVGenWeb Project, "Senseney's Etchings," West Virginia Genealogy, accessed May 25, 2021, https://www.wvgenweb.org/ohio/gsenseney1.jpg.

39 may have developed his technique for printing color etchings in association with Edwards: Charles Marvin Fairchild Memorial Gallery, "Masters in Mezzotint: Color Prints by S. Arlent Edwards," Georgetown University Library, 2003, https://www.library.georgetown.edu/exhibition/masters-mezzotint-color-prints-s-arlent-edwards.

REPRODUCTIONS

44 Jacobi described his working method: Emil Jacobi, "The Gelatine Process," in: Frederick H. Hitchcock (ed.), *The Building of a Book: A Series of Practical Articles,* The Grafton Press, New York, 1906.

46 who later became a prize-winning photographer: https://www.translatetheweb.com/?from=de&to=en&dl=en&a=https://peoplepill.com/people/carl-heinrich-jacobi"Carl Heinrich Jacobi," People Pill, accessed May 25, 2021, https://peoplepill.com/people/carl-heinrich-jacobi.

46 the aristocrat and photography enthusiast, Carlos Relvas: Giaco Furino, "This Odd House Is a Shrine to Early Photography," Vice Magazine, last modified July 27, 2016, https://www.vice.com/en/article/z4qd8x/odd-early-photography-shrine-portugal-casa-relvas.

47 The Taber-Prang Art Co. of Springfield, Massachusetts, reproduced these two 1914 images: Taber-Prang Art Company, "Illustrated Catalog," Web Archive, accessed May 25, 2021, [1923],

THE 1925 BROCHURE

50 the American agent for Brewer's 'proofs': "Made Reputation with Etchings of Old World Cathedrals," *St. Joseph Gazette* (St. Joseph, Missouri), April 22, 1928, 27.

INDEX

Artwork titles are in quotes (with makers in parentheses). Page numbers in boldface refer to illustrations.

"Aix La Chapelle (Aachen)" (1911), one of Brewer's early monotone etchings.

"Sorrento (Italy)," a strongly vertical
view completed by Brewer in 1926.

AUTHOR NOTE

Benjamin S. Dunham is a retired music association executive and magazine editor living near Cape Cod in Massachusetts, USA. Because of his wife's family connection to James Alphege Brewer, he began collecting the artist's etchings in 2015 and now researches and manages a well-frequented website about the artist (www.jalphegebrewer.info). When he began, the biographical references on Brewer were sketchy to say the least and often wrong, even with basic facts like when he was born and died and where he lived all of his life. But with the help of online searches, genealogical records, the archives of guilds, clubs, historical societies, and museums, and especially the memories of helpful Brewer and Lucas family members, his story began to come together.

Prior to his 12 years as editor of *Early Music America* magazine (retiring in 2014), Mr. Dunham enjoyed an active career in arts administration and journalism, serving as executive vice president of the U.S. National Music Council, executive director of the American Symphony Orchestra in Carnegie Hall, director of public relations and publications for the American Symphony Orchestra League (now League of American Orchestras), assistant editor of the *Music Educators Journal*, and editor of *American Recorder* magazine. In 1981, as the first executive director of Chamber Music America, he was named "Arts Administrator of the Year" by the *Arts Management* publication. He has served on the boards of the National Guild for Community Arts Education, the American Recorder Society, and the Boston Early Music Festival and was a member of the Avery Fisher Artist Program Recommendation Board. He performed on recorder and viola da gamba in early music ensembles in Washington, D.C., and in the SouthCoast region of Massachusetts and has reviewed concerts and recordings for national and regional media.

ACKNOWLEDGMENTS

In compiling the material for the website and this book, I am grateful to have had the help of many dealers, collectors, researchers, librarians, curators, archivists, friends, and family descendants. These have included Gavin Smith, Robin Turner, Dr. John Carpenter, Gordon Clarke, Peter Jones, Elizabeth Harvey-Lee, June Gould, Dr. Jonathan Oates, Deborah Crown, Margaret Poulton, Carol Griffiths, Alison Saunders, Tom Lynch, Veronica Jacobi, George Gelles, Tim Dayton (Kansas State University), Robert La France (Ball State University), Krystle Satrum (Huntington Library), Richard Morgan, Rachael Daggett, Erik Senseney, Edward Klekowski, Kevin Ogilvie-White, Daisy Morant, Jeffrey B. Miller, and Stephanie Rolfe. Bob Armstrong and Anne Williams provided helpful information about jigsaw puzzles. Kevin Alves (customframingnb.com) has been an important collaborator in framing my Brewer collection. Special thanks are due to John Hughes of Bracebridge Gallery, the archivist of the Fine Art Trade Guild (www.fineart.co.uk), for identifying the many editions of works by members of the Brewer family authorized by the Guild. The Jewish Museum in Frankfurt, Germany, has been gracious in letting me reproduce works by Ludwig Meidner. I have benefited from the services of IndexBusters.com and the eagle-eye reading of Rebecca Hutchinson. The guidance of Jeremy Burbidge and Simon Paterson of Peacock Press has been invaluable as the book has neared publication. Finally, the endearing support and motivational urgings of my wife Wendy and son Sam have been deeply appreciated and critically important at every stage of this fascinating and all-consuming process.